COMPLETE FLAGS
OF THE WORLD

**LONDON, NEW YORK, MELBOURNE,
MUNICH, AND DELHI**

THIS RELAUNCH EDITION

DK LONDON

Senior Editor Simon Mumford
Editor Suhel Ahmed
US Editors Lindsay Walter, Allison Singer
Pre-production Producer Ben Marcus
Producer Vivienne Yong
Flag illustrations and 3-D flag maps
Simon Mumford
Picture Research Martin Copeland
Jacket Designers Laura Brim, Charlie Noon
Jacket Design Development Manager
Sophia MTT

DK DELHI

Senior Editor Neha Gupta
Editor Ishani Nandi
Art Editors Nishesh Batnagar, Shipra Jain,
Nidhi Mehra
Assistant Art Editors Dhirendra Singh,
Shreya Sadhan
Managing Editor Alka Thakur Hazarika
Managing Art Editor Romi Chakraborty
Senior DTP Designer Harish Aggarwal
DTP Designer Jaypal Singh Chauhan
Jacket Designer Suhita Dharamjit

Managing Editor Gareth Jones
Managing Art Editor Philip Letsu
Publisher Andrew Macintyre
Art Director Phil Ormerod
Associate Publishing Director Liz Wheeler
Publishing Director Jonathan Metcalf

The original edition of this book was produced in association with The Flag Institute, UK.
We would like to dedicate this book to the late Dr. William G. Crampton, Director of
the Flag Institute, without whom it would not have been possible.
Vexillology artwork and consultants Graham Bartram, Michael Faul

First published in the United States in 1997 as *The Ultimate Pocket Flags of the World*
by DK Publishing, 4th Floor, 345 Hudson Street, New York, New York 10014

4 6 8 10 9 7 5

006-196332-May 2014

Reprinted with Revisions 1998, Second Edition 1999, Third Edition 2002, Fourth Edition 2005,
Reprinted with Revisions 2006, Fifth Edition 2008, Relaunched Sixth Edition 2014.

Published in Great Britain by Dorling Kindersley Limited.
A catalog record for this book is available from the Library of Congress.

ISBN: 978-1-4654-1967-5

DK books are available at special discounts when purchased in bulk for sales promotions, premiums,
fund-raising, or educational use. For details, contact: DK Publishing Special Markets, 4th Floor,
345 Hudson Street, New York, New York 10014 or SpecialSales@dk.com.

Printed and bound in Hong Kong

Discover more at **www.dk.com**

COMPLETE
FLAGS
OF THE WORLD

Contents

AUSTRALASIA & OCEANIA

ASIA

Flag directory

Flag directory (continued)

A brief history of flags

Flags are a part of everyday life. They are used by countries, provinces, cities, international bodies, organizations, and companies. Flags are a potent symbol of a country's nationhood, and their design is often closely interwoven with the history and struggles endured by its people to establish a national identity or to gain its independence. A country's flag is therefore often a huge source of pride and a focal point for the historical, social, and geographical elements that define a nation.

EARLY FLAGS

The earliest known flags were used in China, to identify different parts of the army. The ancient civilizations of Greece, Rome, and the Middle East used them in similar ways, but it was the Romans who made most use of these symbols. Each unit of their army had its own standard, including the famous eagles of the legions. The Romans also introduced the first true flag in the western world—the *vexillum*, a square flag used by their cavalry, from which the term "vexillology"—the study of flags—originates. The *vexillum* did not resemble a modern flag because it was fixed to a horizontal pole. Flags attached to one side of an upright pole were introduced to the West by the Arabs in the 1st century, and flags with actual designs on them became widespread during the Crusades.

An early Roman *vexillum*, the first true flag

Flag bears the name of the legion

CHINESE PIRATE FLAG

For centuries, piracy was prevalent on the South China Seas, with most pirate ships hoisting flags to bring them good fortune. These flags were often beautifully drawn and tended to depict gods and goddesses who were thought to rule the waves.

An early version of a Chinese pirate flag depicting the goddess T'ien Hou

The heraldic family banner of British prime minister Sir Winston Churchill

The shield is the focal point of the armorial bearings

The lion is the crest of the Churchill family

HERALDRY

In the Middle Ages, heraldry—the art of producing and recording coats of arms—became a popular means of identifying kings and noblemen. Since then, heraldry has influenced flags greatly, laying down rules for their design and use, and creating new flag types. Owners of coats of arms often had heraldic flags made for them, which were used to symbolize their power and authority. Traditionally there are four types: the long *standard*, the rectangular *banner*, the *badge-flag*, and the *pennon*. A coat of arms consists of the following parts: a shield, which can contain symbols relevant to the history of the bearer's family; supporters (a human or animal figure) on either side of the shield; a helmet with a wreath; mantling (the strips of cloth hanging from the wreath); and a crest on top of the shield. There may also be a scroll displaying a motto.

FLAGS FOR IDENTIFICATION

Since the days of the first warships and the earliest trading vessels, flags have been used at sea. Today such ships—as well as passenger vessels and other boats used for recreation—still use flags. Many flag traditions started out at sea, including ships raising the national flag of the country at whose port they are arriving, which is known as flying a "courtesy flag."

On leaving port, many ships hoist the blue flag with a white square in the center, called the Blue Peter.

SIGNALING WITH FLAGS

One of the oldest uses for flags is for signaling between ships at sea. In the wars between the Greeks and Persians (547–478 BCE), signals were made by both sides with flaglike objects called "vexilloids." The first system of flag signals to use letters and numbers dates from the 17th century, which evolved into semaphore signaling in the 19th century. Mariners relied on semapohores during this period because it was the fastest means of communication between vessels.

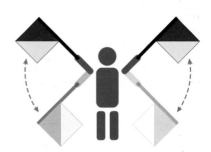

Semaphore flags are used for signaling between ships at sea

A brief history of flags (continued)

FLAGS IN POLITICS

With the growth of independent nation states, flags have become more important in politics. Many newly independent states choose flags based on the political parties that secured their independence. Revolutionary movements usually have their own flags, and private and professional organizations are also increasingly adopting flags.

Flags in the political arena can become very potent symbols to harness and mobilize public support. Historically, the socialist movement has used red in its flags to represent its cause (the color has been associated with left-wing politics since the French Revolution). The anarchist movement, meanwhile, is well-known for using a black flag. One of the most common symbols to represent peace and togetherness is a rainbow. The international environmental organization Greenpeace, for example, has adopted the motif in its flag to symbolize its determination to protect the environment by peaceful means.

The symbol of a rainbow in flags promotes the idea of peace and togetherness

FLAGS IN SPORT

Flags are used for signaling and identification in many sports, including motorsports, golf, gymnastics, skiing, cross-country events, and team sports such as baseball and football. They are employed as signals, markers, and as decorations. In addition, both individual and national teams have their own flags bearing their colors and badge, which help them and their fans form a collective identity.

Motorsports fans wave flags in the stands to show support for their favorite teams

NASA astronaut John W. Young salutes the US flag during the Apollo 16 moon landing

Reciprocally, sports fans wave flags in the stands to show their support for their team, and, in individual sports, fans will indicate their support for a player by waving the flag of his or her home country. Flags are also used to signal the beginning and ending of certain sporting events. Each Olympic Games, for example, has its own flag, as well as the Olympic Standard (the flag bearing the five colored rings), which are both raised and lowered to mark the opening and closing of the Games. In addition, when medals are presented to the victors at the Olympics, their national flags are raised to celebrate the achievement.

KEY FLAGS IN WORLD HISTORY

Throughout history, certain flags have provided the inspiration for the design of others, starting with the American Stars and Stripes of 1777, which has inspired more flags than any other. A similar degree of influence has been exerted by the French *Tricolore* from 1794, giving rise to the Dutch flag and its major derivative, the Russian Tricolor, which in turn formed the basis of most of the flags of the countries in eastern Europe.

SECTIONS OF THIS BOOK

This book deals predominantly with national, international, and subnational flags, as well as national coats of arms, and is arranged continent by continent. Among national flags are the state ensign and state flag, for government use only on sea and land; the civil ensign and civil flag, for private and commercial use, and the naval ensign, flown by warships. Subnational flags may be of states (US), provinces (Canada), cantons (Switzerland), and overseas territories or other such areas. The book also includes a section on flags adopted by international organizations, and finally offers a listing of flag signals and semaphore.

Parts of the flag

The study of flags is known as "vexillology." Over the years, vexillologists have established a set of flag terminologies to describe the parts, patterns, and other elements that make up a modern-day flag. The diagram below illustrates the main parts of a flag. Many of these terms are used throughout the book in the detailed flag descriptions.

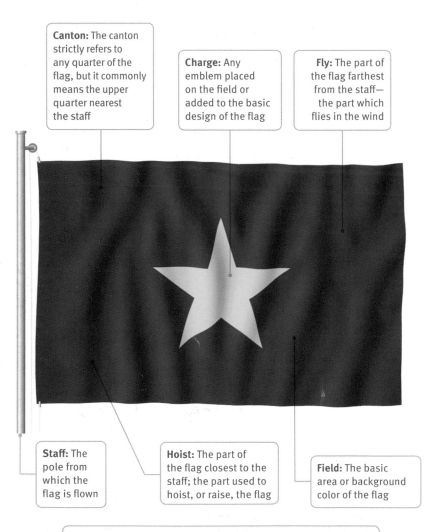

Canton: The canton strictly refers to any quarter of the flag, but it commonly means the upper quarter nearest the staff

Charge: Any emblem placed on the field or added to the basic design of the flag

Fly: The part of the flag farthest from the staff— the part which flies in the wind

Staff: The pole from which the flag is flown

Hoist: The part of the flag closest to the staff; the part used to hoist, or raise, the flag

Field: The basic area or background color of the flag

Ratio describes the relative proportions of height against width. For example, ratio: 1:2 represents a flag twice as wide as it is high.

Heraldic terms

Heraldry is the art of producing and recording coats of arms. The practice of heraldry is nearly 900 years old and has had a great influence on flags, creating new kinds of flags and laying down the ground rules for their design and use. The diagram below describes the main elements that are usually included in a coat of arms.

Crest: The element that appears at the extreme top of the arms, above the shield

Wreath or Torse: The rope of colors placed above the helmet or shield

Mantling: The strips of cloth hanging or flying from the wreath

Chief: The top third of the shield

Supporters: The figures, human or animal that hold the shield

Scroll: The strip—usually below the shield—that contains the motto

Shield: The basic unit on which the coat of arms is portrayed

Compartment: The base, often a mound, on which the shield stands

TO·LEAD·IS·TO·SERVE

Flag colors

RED: SYMBOLIC USES

Flag colors generally carry symbolic meaning. Red is one of the most commonly used colors and traditionally represents strength, bravery, revolution, hardiness, and bloodshed. Below are some examples.

Albania: strength and valor at war

China: the Communist revolution

Kyrgyzstan: the valor of *Manas* the *Noble*

Morocco: descent of royal *Alaouite* family

Tunisia: blood shed in 1574 Turkish conquest

Turkey: the south (origin of its founders)

GREEN: SYMBOLIC USES

Green is traditionally a healing color, and is often used to represent nature, agriculture, and fertility, as well as other positive themes such as hope and love. It is also the color of Islam as it recalls the Prophet Muhammad's favorite color.

Brazil: the reigning house of Braganza

Mauritania: Islam; bright future and growth

Pakistan: Islam; hope, joy, and love

Saudi Arabia: the Muslim Wahabi sect

Turkmenistan: life, prosperity, and peace

Zambia: lush flora and rich natural resources

BLUE: SYMBOLIC USES

Blue is universally associated with water and sky. In flags, the color has historically symbolized justice, prosperity, and perseverance. Island nations, or those with an extensive coastline, often feature blue as a key part of their flag design.

Botswana: water (a resource for agriculture)

El Salvador: *añil* (a source for indigo dye)

Kazakhstan: cultural and ethnic unity

Micronesia: Pacific Ocean; UN flag

Somalia: sky and Indian Ocean

St. Lucia: Caribbean Sea and Atlantic Ocean

YELLOW: SYMBOLIC USES

Yellow typically represents the sun, wealth, and plentitude. The color appears in many flags of African nations, often to denote that the land is bathed in sunshine. Agricultural prosperity and crops are also symbolized with yellow.

Bhutan: civil tradition and temporal authority

Brunei: royalty (Sultan of Brunei)

Columbia: sunshine; the abundance of gold

Ecuador: crops and fertile soil

Grenada: wisdom and wealth

Ukraine: *Kupola* (the domes of its churches)

Flag colors (continued)

BLACK: SYMBOLIC USES

Black usually carries a strong or serious message often linked to a period of struggle. In flags, the shade has been used to symbolize determination, ethnic heritage, and the fortitude required to defeat one's enemies.

Afghanistan: a troubled past pre-independence

Angola: the African continent it belongs to

Estonia: fertile soil; Estonia's dark history

Iraq: determination in the face of adversity

Libya: Senussi Dynasty of 1837; resistance

Papua New Guinea: native art and clothing

WHITE: SYMBOLIC USES

A plain white flag is the universal symbol for truce. Usually, white flags traditionally represent aspirational themes such as peace, purity, and innocence. However, in some countries it is the color of mourning.

Algeria: peace (after Algerian War 1954–62)

Cyprus: peace (between Turks and Greeks)

Finland: snow (covering the land in winter)

Israel: light, honesty, and innocence

Singapore: everlasting purity and virtue

South Korea: purity and peace

PAN-AFRICAN COLORS: SYMBOLIC USES

Pan-Africanism is the concept that African countries should embrace their mutual bond as Africans. Red, yellow, green, and black are colors commonly used to represent Pan-Africanism. These colors have important individual meanings.

Benin

Ethiopia

Ghana

Guinea-Bissau

Red: the blood uniting all people of black African ancestry

Yellow: a reference to the sun; the presence of precious resources, particularly gold

Green: the abundant flora and natural wealth of Africa

Black: a symbol of the African race

PAN-ARABIC COLORS: SYMBOLIC USES

The Pan-Arabic colors are black, white, green, and red. They were first combined in the flag of the Arab revolt in 1916. Each of the Pan-Arabic colors is meant to represent a specific Arab dynasty, or era. The eras are listed below.

Iran

Jordan

Kuwait

United Arab Emirates

Black: Abbasid Caliphate (750–1258 AD)

White: Ummayad Caliphate (661–750 AD)

Green: Fatimid Caliphate (909–1171 AD)

Red: rulers of the Maghreb and Al-Adalus (647–732 AD)

Types of flags

Tricolor

A flag of three stripes of three colors, either horizontal or vertical.

Tribar

A flag of three stripes of two colors, horizontal or vertical.

Bicolor

A flag of two stripes of different colors, either horizontal or vertical.

Cross

A cross is vertical, centrally placed, and extends across the whole flag.

Scandinavian cross

A cross with the upright set closer to the hoist than to the fly.

Bend

A flag divided by a diagonal strip.

Saltire

A diagonal cross stretching from corner to corner of the flag.

Triangle

A flag divided by a triangle of a different color, usually at the hoist.

Serration

A narrow strip of color separating two broader stripes or larger areas.

Canton

A flag charged with a design in the corner, usually at the hoist.

Quartered

A flag divided into four equal sections of differing design.

Bordered

A flag where the central color is surrounded by a different color.

Flag identification guide

The flags in this guide have been grouped into the various design types found in vexillology (see pp.20–21). Within each category they have been arranged by color, starting with the color that is most common in the group.

It is interesting to note that many neighboring countries have flags with similar colors and design elements, though sometimes the opposite is true. The final group contains flags that share the traits of several design types.

TRICOLOR

Netherlands (p.170)

Luxembourg (p.187)

Croatia (p.215)

Russian Federation (p.228)

Slovakia (p.213)

Slovenia (p.214)

Paraguay (p.95)

Serbia (p.218)

France (p.186)

Niger (p.117)

India (p.264)

Ivory Coast (p.128)

Ireland (p.175)

Hungary (p.211)

Bulgaria (p.222)

Iran (p.253)

Italy (p.196)

Mexico (p.57)

Yemen (p.246)

Egypt (p.104)

TRICOLOR (continued)

Syria (p.241) **Iraq** (p.252) **Libya** (p.103) **Malawi** (p.142)

Kenya (p.112) **Afghanistan** (p.260) **Germany** (p.165) **Belgium** (p.174)

Bolivia (p.94) **Ghana** (p.130) **Lithuania** (p.163) **Myanmar** (p.268)

Ethiopia (p.109) **Guinea** (p.125) **Mali** (p.120) **Senegal** (p.121)

Cameroon (p.134) **Colombia** (p.80) **Ecuador** (p.84) **Venezuela** (p.81)

Chad (p.118) **Romania** (p.224) **Andorra** (p.189) **Moldova** (p.225)

Flag identification guide (continued)

 TRICOLOR (continued)

Sierra Leone (p.126)

Uzbekistan (p.255)

Tajikistan (p.259)

Lesotho (p.147)

Estonia (p.161)

Gabon (p.137)

Rwanada (p.113)

St. Vincent & Grenadines (p.74)

Azerbaijan (p.236)

Armenia (p.237)

 TRIBAR

Austria (p.208)

Lebanon (p.240)

Canada (p.34)

Peru (p.85)

Latvia (p.162)

Nicaragua (p.62)

El Salvador (p.60)

Honduras (p.61)

Argentina (p.97)

Guatemala (p.58)

Nigeria (p.133)

Spain (p.191)

TRIBAR (continued)

Cambodia (p.271)

Laos (p.270)

Mongolia (p.257)

Barbados (p.75)

 BICOLOR

Indonesia (p.278)

Monaco (p.188)

Singapore
(p.280)

Poland (p.164)

Malta (p.197)

Burkina (p.129)

Belarus (p.226)

Portugal (p.190)

Algeria (p.101)

San Marino
(p.199)

Haiti (p.68)

Liechtenstein
(p.207)

Angola (p.139)

Vatican City
(p.198)

Ukraine (p.227)

Pakistan (p.261)

Flag identification guide (continued)

 CROSS

Switzerland (p.200)

Georgia (p.239)

Dominican Republic (p.69)

Dominica (p.72)

 SCANDINAVIAN CROSS

Denmark (p.158)

Norway (p.157)

Iceland (p.156)

Sweden (p.159)

Finland (p.160)

 BEND

Congo (p.138)

St. Kitts & Nevis (p.70)

Tanzania (p.141)

Solomon Islands (p.296)

Namibia (p.145)

Dem. Rep. of Congo (p.116)

Trinidad & Tobago (p.77)

Brunei (p.281)

SALTIRE

Burundi (p.114)

Jamaica (p.65)

 TRIANGLE

Czech Republic
(p.212)

Philippines
(p.282)

Cuba (p.66)

Djibouti (p.108)

**Equatorial
Guinea** (p.135)

Sudan (p.105)

Jordan (p.244)

South Sudan
(p.106)

South Africa
(p.149)

Vanuatu (p.293)

East Timor
(p.279)

Guyana (p.82)

**São Tomé &
Príncipe** (p.136)

Zimbabwe
(p.143)

Mozambique
(p.144)

Comoros (p.151)

Bahamas (p.67)

Eritrea (p.107)

Flag identification guide (continued)

 SERRATION

Bahrain (p.250)

Qatar (p.249)

 CANTON

Chile (p.93)

Taiwan (p.283)

Samoa (p.303)

Tonga (p.304)

USA (p.39)

Liberia (p.127)

Malaysia (p.273)

Australia (p.290)

New Zealand (p.305)

Tuvalu (p.302)

Fiji (p.294)

Greece (p.223)

Uruguay (p.96)

Togo (p.131)

QUARTERED

Panama (p.64)

BORDERED

Montenegro (p.217)

Maldives (p.265)

Grenada (p.76)

Sri Lanka (p.266)

PLAIN WITH EMBLEM

Vietnam (p.272)

China (p.284)

Kyrgyzstan (p.258)

Morocco (p.100)

Turkey (p.238)

Tunisia (p.102)

Albania (p.220)

Bangladesh (p.267)

Brazil (p.86)

Mauritania (p.119)

Zambia (p.140)

Saudi Arabia (p.245)

Flag identification guide (continued)

 PLAIN WITH EMBLEM (continued)

St. Lucia (p.73)

Palau (p.297)

Somalia (p.110)

Micronesia (p.298)

Kosovo (p.219)

Japan (p.287)

South Korea (p.286)

Cyprus (p.242)

 OTHER TYPES

Israel (p.243)

Costa Rica (p.63)

Thailand (p.269)

North Korea (p.285)

Cape Verde (p.123)

Belize (p.59)

Botswana (p.146)

Kiribati (p.301)

United Kingdom (p.176)

Swaziland (p.148)

Nauru (p.300)

Kazakhstan (p.256)

OTHER TYPES (continued)

**Bosnia &
Herzegovina**
(p.216)

Marshall Islands
(p.299)

Mauritius (p.153)

Gambia (p.122)

**Central African
Republic** (p.115)

Seychelles
(p.150)

Benin (p.132)

Guinea Bissau
(p.124)

UAE (p.248)

Kuwait (p.251)

Oman (p.247)

Madagascar
(p.152)

Suriname (p.83)

Turkmenistan
(p.254)

**Antigua &
Barbuda** (p.71)

**Papua New
Guinea** (p.295)

Uganda (p.111)

Macedonia
(p.221)

Bhutan (p.263)

Nepal (p.262)

North America

Canada

Adopted February 15, 1965 | **Ratio** 1:2 | **Usage** National and Civil

Red represents the sacrifice made by Canadians during the First World War

White represents the snowy north of Canada

A stylized maple leaf has been Canada's national emblem for over 150 years

Canada became a nation in 1867 when four colonies united. Later, six other provinces and two territories joined the Confederation.

The Royal Standard shows the Arms of Canada, with the personal emblem of Queen Elizabeth II. The quarters show the arms of England, Scotland, Ireland, and France, the historical origin for the majority of European settlers to Canada. The lowest stripe shows the red maple leaf, which is Canada's national emblem.

THE NEW MAPLE LEAF FLAG

An earlier flag, the "Pearson's Pennant," did not meet with universal approval. A new consensus, based on the maple leaf and national color, resulted in the "Maple Leaf Flag," which was adopted by Parliament in 1965. The Union Flag is often flown to show Canada's links with the United Kingdom.

CANADIAN ROYAL STANDARD

The maple leaves represent Canada's national emblem

The quarters of the shield represent England, Scotland, Ireland, and France—the homelands of many Canadian people

Provincial and official flags

The date when each province joined the Confederation is shown next to the province name.

Alberta 1905

The shield dates from 1907 and was placed on a blue field to make a flag in 1967. The shield depicts a scene from the vast wheat lands of the west under St. George's Cross.

British Columbia 1871

This flag, adopted in 1960, is an armorial banner of the arms, granted in 1906. The sun placed over heraldic waters represents the province's position on the west coast.

Manitoba 1870

The flag is intended to recall and to preserve the old Canadian Red Ensign, with Manitoba's shield, depicting a buffalo on a rock, in the fly. It was adopted in 1966.

New Brunswick 1867

Another armorial banner, authorized in 1965. The galley ship represents shipbuilding, once an important industry, and the lion represents New Brunswick's ties with Britain.

Provincial and official flags

Newfoundland & Labrador 1949

The colors of the flag represent all aspects of the province, such as snow, ice, and the sea. The design is intended to recall the Union Jack, the territory's previous flag.

Northwest Territories 1870

The flag was a competition winner in 1969. It contains the shield from the arms adopted in 1956. The lakes are represented by blue, and snow by white.

Nova Scotia 1867

This flag is theoretically the oldest flag of a British Dominion. "Nova Scotia" means "New Scotland." Its flag has a St. Andrew's Cross in reversed colors, with the Scottish Royal Arms.

Nunavut 1999

The figure on this flag symbolizes the stone monuments used to mark sacred places. The North Star represents the leadership of the community's elders.

Ontario 1867

The flag was adopted in 1965 and also attempts to recall and preserve the Canadian Red Ensign. The shield is from the arms of 1868 and was the first design to use a maple leaf.

Prince Edward Island 1873

The flag is a banner of the arms granted in 1905. It depicts an island, with a great British oak and its "descendants," under the protection of a British lion.

Quebec 1867

Adopled in 1948, this flag is a modern version of the *Fleurdelysé*, an old French-Canadian flag. The *fleur-de-lis* flower is symbolic of France.

Saskatchewan 1905

Adopted in 1969, the flag combines the provincial shield (representing forests and grain) with the floral emblem—the western red lily.

Provincial and official flags (continued)

Yukon Territory 1898

Accepted in 1967, the flag uses the 1956 coat of arms. Forests, snows, and waters are symbolized by the colors.

Cape Breton Island 1994

This competition-winning flag was adopted in 1994 by Cape Breton in Nova Scotia. The bird is a bald eagle.

Labrador 1973

The spruce sprigs on this regional flag denote the three races of the larger Newfoundland & Labrador Province.

Governor-General of Canada 1981

This flag, dating from 1981, does not use the British Royal Crest; it has its own crest of a lion holding up a maple leaf.

United States of America

Adopted July 4, 1960 | **Ratio** 10:19 | **Usage** National and Civil

The 50 stars stand for each of the current states of the Union

13 stripes stand for the original 13 colonies, which formed the US

If a new state joins the Union, a star is added the following July 4

The US was formed when 13 colonies rose against the British in 1775. They declared their independence from Britain on July 4, 1776.

The first flag used by the Americans was an adaptation of the British Red Ensign, known as the "Grand Union Flag" (see p.40). From this developed the distinctive "Stars and Stripes," as it is known today, which still has the 13 stripes for each of the original colonies to join the Union, and a star for each state, which is now part of the US. The latest star was added on July 4, 1960, after Hawaii joined the US in 1959.

A TRULY NATIONAL FLAG

The flag of 1777 (see p.40), marked a break with old colonial ties. It became the first of a new kind of flag, one that was truly a national flag in the modern sense. Its basic design and color combination was soon copied by other new nations.

The Stars and Stripes is an all-purpose flag, but the US is rich in flags of many other kinds.

THE PRESIDENT'S STANDARD

The presidential standard, in use today, contains the President's version of the national arms, and a ring of 50 stars. The coat of arms depicts a spread eagle holding a shield in the style of the Stars and Stripes, 13 arrows, and 13 olive leaves, indicating the country is prepared for either war or peace. The motto "*E Pluribus Unum*" meaning "Out of many, one," reflects the federal nature of the United States of America.

US: Historical flags

The flags of the Revolutionary and the Civil War still have an influence on the American flags of today.

The Grand Union Flag

The first American flag was adapted from the British Red Ensign of the time. It was known as the "Grand Union Flag," i.e. of the union of 13 colonies. These were represented by the 13 stripes of red and white. The flag was introduced in December 1775 for use on land and at sea.

The Flag of 1795

When two new states joined the Union in 1795, two new stars and two new stripes were added to the flag, making 15 stripes and 15 stars. This set a precedent for adding new stripes and stars when each new state joined the Union. The flag soon became known as the "Star-Spangled Banner."

The Stars and Bars

When the southern states seceded from the Union in 1860, a new flag for the Confederacy was hoisted on March 4, 1861. Known as the "Stars and Bars," it originally had 7 stars, but these increased to 13 in the course of 1861, as more states joined the Confederacy.

The first Stars and Stripes

On June 14, 1777, the Union Jack was removed from the flag in favor of a blue canton with 13 stars, representing a new constellation, which now also represented the United States of America. This was the first use of stars in this way, and set a precedent for many later flags.

The Flag of 1818

Five new states were formed after 1795, but a new flag was not designed until 1817, when Congress decreed that in order to preserve the appearance of the flag, in future only new stars would be added and it would revert to 13 stripes. The new stars were added on July 4, 1818, and this system has been followed ever since.

The Battle Flag or "Flag of the South"

The Battle Flag with its distinctive saltire on a red field (Southern Cross) was introduced in September 1861, specifically for use in battle. On land it was square with a white border, but the rectangular naval version, without a border, is now accepted as "The Flag of the South."

State flags

The date when each state joined the Union is shown beside the state name.

Alabama 1819

This flag, which was adopted in 1895, shows a red saltire on a white field. It is intended to recall the Southern Cross or Battle Flag of the Confederate States.

Alaska 1959

The flag was designed by a Native American schoolboy in 1926, when Alaska was still a territory. It depicts the Big Dipper and the northern Pole star. Gold also represents Alaska's mineral reserves.

Arizona 1912

The red and yellow rays recall the period of Spanish rule, and the copper star represents mineral riches. The flag was designed locally and adopted in 1927.

Arkansas 1836

The flag recalls the Southern Cross. The lower stars represent former colonial powers and the upper star stands for the Confederacy. The flag was adopted in 1913.

California 1850

The flag is based on that of the California Republic declared at Sonora in 1846; it did not become the state flag until 1911. It depicts a grizzly bear and a star representing freedom.

Colorado 1876

The C-shaped emblem contains the colors of Spain, which once laid claim to this area. The gold ball also represents the state's mineral riches. The flag was adopted in 1911.

Connecticut 1788

The arms date back to the seal of 1784, and the blue field to the Civil War period, when the flag was a Union color. This design was adopted in 1897.

Delaware 1787

The arms date back to 1777 and the flag, adopted in 1913, includes the date Delaware joined the Union. The colors recall the uniforms worn during the Revolutionary War.

State flags (continued)

Florida 1845

This is another flag which recalls the Southern Cross used by the Confederacy during the Civil War. The original flag, adopted in 1868, had only the seal; the red saltire was added in 1900.

Georgia 1788

The revised state flag for Georgia was introduced in 2003, following objections to the inclusion of the Confederate flag on the previous two designs. The three bars evoke pre-1956 versions of the flag.

Hawaii 1959

The state flag, originally representing the independent kingdom, was adopted in 1845. The Union Jack recalls a flag given to the King by an army officer in 1793. The stripes stand for the main islands.

Idaho 1890

The flag, originally a military color, bears the state seal in the center; beneath it is a scroll with the state's name. The flag in this form was adopted in 1927, with new specifications in 1957.

Illinois 1818

Created in 1915, the central emblem of the Illinois flag, depicts elements from the state seal, including a bald eagle and a shield of the Stars and Stripes. The name was added beneath this in 1970.

Indiana 1816

The flag was the winning entry in a design competition held in 1916, and was officially adopted in 1917. The stars in the outside circle are for the original states and bottom arc is for the subsequent ones.

Iowa 1846

The red, white, and blue colors stand for French Louisiana, of which Iowa was once a part. In the center is the seal of 1847. The flag was adopted in this form in 1921.

Kansas 1861

The flag of Kansas follows a very common seal and name pattern. The original flag of 1925 had the seal, recalling settlement and agriculture, and a sunflower—the state flower. The name was added in 1963.

State flags (continued)

Kentucky 1792

This is another flag derived from the militia colors. The flag was adopted in 1918 and regularized in 1962. Like many state flags, it contains the seal, the state name, and a wreath of goldenrod—the state flower.

Louisiana 1812

The pelican, representing self-sacrifice and the state's role as a protector, has long been the badge of Louisiana, but the flag was only adopted in 1912 and slightly modified in 2004. The Acadians, or "Cajuns," also have their own flag.

Maine 1820

The flag dates from 1909 when the arms, adopted in 1820, were placed on a blue field. The star and motto recall Maine's northerly location. It was the northernmost state of the Union, until Michigan joined in 1837.

Maryland 1788

This is the only flag which is a true heraldic banner, reproducing the arms of the Baltimore family, once the "proprietors" of the state. Each side of the family is represented by two quarters. It was adopted in 1904.

Massachusetts 1788

The flag was originally adopted in 1908 and revised in 1971, replacing a pine tree with the coat of arms adopted in 1780. The arms, depicting a Native American holding a bow, now appears on both sides of the flag.

Michigan 1837

The arms was adopted in 1832, and placed on a blue field to make the state flag in 1911. The mottoes translate to "I will defend," and "If you seek a pleasant peninsula, look about you."

Minnesota 1858

The motto on this flag, "The North Star," was retained from when the state was the northernmost in the Union. The flag was originally adopted in 1893 and revised in 1957.

Mississippi 1817

The flag of Mississippi was adopted in 1894. It combines both the Confederacy's Southern Cross with the stripes of its first flag, the Stars and Bars, however on the flag of Mississippi, the upper stripe is blue.

State flags (continued)

Missouri 1821

The colors of the flag recall when the region was under French control. The 24 stars stand for Missouri being the 24th state to join the Union. Within the seal itself are another 24 stars. The flag was adopted in 1913.

Montana 1889

The flag is derived from the former state militia colors, while the motto, "Gold and Silver," is in Spanish, recalling Spain's claim to the area. The flag was adopted in 1905 and had the name added in 1981.

Nebraska 1867

The flag of Nebraska was adopted in 1925 and uses the seal which was adopted in 1867. This depicts an allegorical landscape, symbolic of the state's agricultural and industrial development.

Nevada 1864

The flag emerged from a design competition and was adopted in 1929. It was revised in 1991, and the state name was placed underneath the boughs of the sagebrush and the star, which represents the state.

New Hampshire 1788

The design was adopted in 1909, making use of the seal, which dates back to 1775. It depicts a ship, the *Raleigh*, being built on the docks of the town of Portsmouth during the Revolutionary War.

New Jersey 1787

The buff field recalls the uniforms worn during the Revolutionary War. The flag with the arms was adopted in 1896 and made widely available in 1938.

New Mexico 1912

This most distinctive flag was adopted in 1925 and uses the sun symbol of the *Zia Pueblo* Indians, while the colors represent the Spanish colonial era.

New York 1788

The flag dates originally from flags used in the Revolutionary War, but in this form only from 1901. Prior to that the flag had a buff field. The two figures symbolize liberty and justice. The coat of arms dates from 1777.

State flags (continued)

North Carolina 1789

The original flag was adopted in 1861 at the outbreak of the Civil War, and was in the same colors as the Stars and Bars. The present design dates from 1885. It contains the initials of the state in the blue stripe.

North Dakota 1889

The flag was originally used by the state militia—the North Dakota Infantry—and was adopted in 1911, almost without alteration, explaining its squarish shape. A version of the national arms is in the center.

Ohio 1803

The pennant-shaped flag of Ohio is derived from a cavalry guidon of the Civil War period. The 17 stars recall that Ohio was the 17th state to join the Union, and the circle or "O" refers to the state's initial.

Oklahoma 1907

The basic design emerged from a design competition and was adopted in 1925. The name was added in 1941. The Native American emblems, all symbols of peace, recall the previous name, "Indian Territory."

Oregon 1859

This is now the only state flag with a different design on its reverse. The obverse shows the seal within 33 stars, the state's name, and its date of admission. The reverse shows a beaver. It was adopted in 1925.

Pennsylvania 1787

The coat of arms of the state was adopted in 1777 and regularized in 1875. It was placed on a blue field to make the flag in 1907. The shield is supported by two horses.

Rhode Island 1790

The anchor, symbolic of hope, has long been the emblem of Rhode Island. The flag, based on a Revolutionary War flag, was adopted in 1877 and modified in 1897.

South Carolina 1788

The flag was adopted in 1861 at the very start of the Civil War, but contains emblems used during the Revolutionary War and also used in the state arms. The central palmetto is the state tree.

State flags (continued)

South Dakota 1889

The flag of South Dakota was adopted in 1963 on the basis of previous models, and had the former motto "The Sunshine State" around the seal. This was changed to "The Mount Rushmore State" in 1992.

Tennessee 1796

The three stars represent the three geographical divisions of the state, while its general appearance recalls the Battle Flag or Southern Cross. The flag was adopted in 1905.

Texas 1845

The flag copies the colors of the Stars and Stripes, but with only one star, which dates back to the one found on the plain blue flag of the Republic of Texas. It was adopted in 1839 and retained after Texas joined the Union.

Utah 1896

The beehive in the flag recalls the emblem of the provisional Mormon state of Deseret, located in Utah, and the date recalls their settlement of the region. The present flag dates from 1911 and uses the seal adopted in 1896.

Vermont 1791

The arms, including the Lone Pine emblem, date back to when Vermont was independent from 1777–91. The present flag, based on the former militia flag, was adopted in 1923. The state name appears on a scroll.

Virginia 1788

The state arms was adopted in 1776. The seal, showing Liberty Triumphing over Tyranny, was placed on the flag in 1861 at the start of the Civil War. The design has been used ever since.

Washington 1889

Washington is known as "The Evergreen State," and this is reflected by its flag. It is the only state with a green flag. The seal dates from 1889 and was placed on the flag in 1923.

West Virginia 1863

The coat of arms dates from 1863 when West Virginia seceded from Virginia. The current version of the flag was adopted in 1929 and has the arms within a wreath of rhododendron, the state flower.

State and Overseas Territory flags

The date when each state joined the Union is shown against the state name.

Wisconsin 1848

The flag is derived from the militia colors of the Union in 1863. It depicts the state seal, supported by a miner and a sailor. The shield also recalls mining and sailing. The name and the date were added in 1980.

Wyoming 1890

The flag emerged from a design competition and was adopted in 1917. The flag has been revised several times; at one time the buffalo containing the arms faced the fly. The colors recall the national flag.

District of Columbia 1791

The flag of the Federal District of Columbia is based on a banner of the arms of the Washington family, which originated in England and dates back to 1592. It was adopted in 1938 by a Congress Commission.

American Samoa 1900

A self-governing US dependency, American Samoa's flag shows its links with the guardian state, in the colors and the American bald eagle. Here the eagle carries Samoan emblems.

Guam 1917

The flag was designed locally and adopted in 1917. In the center of the flag, in the US colors, is the seal of the territory, which depicts an idealized landscape. The flag can only be flown with the US flag.

Northern Mariana Islands 1972

The original flag was adopted in 1972, but has undergone several modifications, including the addition of the flower-wreath. It also depicts a gray latte stone, representing the islands' Chamorro culture.

Puerto Rico 1952

The resemblance of this flag to that of Cuba is no coincidence, since the two were designed at the same time, by the same activists. This version was adopted in 1952.

Virgin Islands (US) 1921

The flag dates from 1921 and uses part of the US seal, with the initials of the islands. The three arrows in one claw stand for the main islands; in the other claw is an olive branch.

Military flags

US Army 1956

The flag bears a blue replica of the War Office Seal on a white field. It was officially adopted by President Eisenhower. The date 1775 underneath the banner refers to the year the army was formed.

US Air Force 1951

The flag includes the coat of arms of the US Air force, the Air Force Seal, and 13 stars representing the 13 original colonies. The version of the flag that is used for parades has a gold border.

US Navy 1959

The flag bears the seal of the US Navy on a dark blue field and has a yellow banner underneath inscribed with "United States Navy." The flag is flown in the Navy's offices, during parades, and on other ceremonial occasions.

US Marines 1939

The gold and scarlet colors of the flag are also the official colors of the Marines Corps. The flag bears the Corps' emblem in the center, and is also known as the "Battle Color." The flag is used to represent the Corps' units and formations.

US Coast Guard 1964

The flag bears the Great Seal of the USA on a white field. It is used in parades and ceremonies. The Coast Guard motto "*Semper Paratus,*" which appears at the bottom of the flag, means "Always Ready."

Mexico

Adopted November 2, 1821 | **Ratio** 4:7 | **Usage** National and Civil

The basic design is derived from the French *Tricolore*

Red, white, and green are the colors of the national liberation army in Mexico

The coat of arms incorporates the badge of Mexico City

Mexico was conquered by Spain in the 16th century, but broke away in 1821 to form a Central American state. It became a republic in 1822.

France was the inspiration of those who detached Mexico from Spain in 1821 and they devised a new tricolor based on the flag of the liberation army. At that time, the Italian tricolor was not in use.

The coat of arms on the center stripe distinguishes the flag from that of Italy.

THE AZTEC INHERITANCE

The central emblem is the Aztec pictogram for Tenochtitlán (now Mexico City), the center of their empire. It recalls the legend which inspired the Aztecs to settle on what was originally a lake island.

The form of the coat of arms was most recently revised in 1968.

ARMS OF MEXICO

The lake, with an island, represents Tenochtitlán

Ribbon in the national colors

Aztec legend held that they should found their city on the spot where they saw an eagle on a cactus, eating a snake

Guatemala

Adopted August 17, 1871 | **Ratio** 5:8 | **Usage** National and State

Blue and white are the colors of the original flag of the United Provinces of Central America

The coat of arms was adopted in 1968

Guatemala declared independence at the same time as Mexico and, in 1823, became part of a union with the other Central American states.

In Guatemala, the flag of the United Provinces of Central America, horizontal stripes of blue-white-blue, was used until 1851, when a pro-Spanish government added the red and yellow of Spain to the flag. On August 17, 1871, the original colors were restored as vertical stripes, and with Guatemala's own coat of arms.

THE QUETZAL BIRD

The new coat of arms shows the quetzal, Guatemala's most famous bird, standing on a scroll giving the date of the Declaration of Independence. The present form of the arms was adopted in 1968. When used at sea for civil purposes, the flag does not contain the arms.

ARMS OF GUATEMALA

The date of the Declaration of Independence

Rifles and swords represent defence of freedom

The quetzal bird with its distinctive tail feathers is a symbol of liberty

Belize

Adopted September 21, 1981 | **Ratio** 2:3 | **Usage** National and State

Red stripes were added to denote the color of the opposition party

The 50 leaves recall 1950, the year the PUP came to power

The country's coat of arms was granted in 1907

Blue is the party color of the PUP

Belize was originally known as British Honduras, a colony formed in 1862 from settlements on the coast of Guatemala.

British Honduras obtained a coat of arms on January 28, 1907, which formed the basis of the badge used on British ensigns. The coat of arms recalls the logging industry, which first led to British settlement there.

From 1968 onward, an unofficial national flag was in use. It was blue with a modified version of the arms —minus the Union Jack—on a white disk in the center. The colors were those of the People's United Party (pup). Around the arms was a wreath of 50 leaves, recalling 1950, when the PUP came to prominence.

On independence in 1981, the flag was retained, but red stripes were added to stand for the opposition party.

ARMS OF BELIZE

The figures, tools, and the mahogany tree represent the logging industry

Wreath of 50 leaves

National motto—"Sub Umbra Floreo," meaning "I Flourish in the Shade"

El Salvador

Adopted May 17, 1912 | **Ratio** 3:5 | **Usage** National and State

The flag is modeled on the flag of the United Provinces of Central America

The title of the state while it was part of the United Provinces of Central America surrounds the emblem

The emblem is surrounded by five flags, recalling the original five United Provinces of Central America

El Salvador's flag recalls the colors of the United Provinces of Central America, used following independence from Spain in 1823.

The flag of Central America was used as the national flag until 1865, when a flag based on the Stars and Stripes was adopted, with blue and white stripes and a red canton containing nine stars.

In 1912, the original design was readopted, with the arms of El Salvador positioned in the center.

TRIANGLES AND VOLCANOES

The coat of arms is similar to those of the United Provinces of Central America. The emblem is based on the Masonic triangle for equality, and depicts the five original provinces with five volcanoes. Around the triangle are five national flags and a wreath, tied in the national colors.

ARMS OF EL SALVADOR

A triangle representing equality

The Cap of Liberty

The motto of Central America—"Dios, Union, Libertad," meaning "God, Union, Liberty"

Five volcanoes representing the original United Provinces

Honduras

Adopted March 7, 1866 | **Ratio** 1:2 | **Usage** National and Civil

The colors and pattern are the same as the flag of the United Provinces of Central America

Five stars recall the five original members of the United Provinces of Central America

Honduras was one of the Spanish colonies which formed the United Provinces of Central America in 1823. It became independent in 1838.

In 1823, Honduras joined the United Provinces of Central America and adopted their flag. In 1866, it was amended: five blue stars were placed in the center to represent the five original Central American provinces. The state flag has the arms of Honduras in the center in place of the stars.

The arms was created in 1838 and revised in 1935. The central feature is a pyramid in Maya style rising from the sea. Around this is a blue band with the name of the state and the date of the Declaration of Independence. Beneath it is a landscape strewn with allegorical items representing mineral and timber industries.

ARMS OF HONDURAS

The cornucopias are symbolic of prosperity and agricultural wealth

A Maya pyramid

The landscape depicts mines, mining tools, forests, and logging tools

Nicaragua

Adopted September 4, 1908 | **Ratio** 3:5 | **Usage** National and Civil

Apart from the text around the arms, the flag is identical to that of the United Provinces of Central America

Arms of Nicaragua

"*America Central*" recalls the United Provinces of Central America

Nicaragua declared independence from Spain in 1821. It was a member of the United Provinces of Central America from 1823 to 1838.

The flag and the arms of Nicaragua in use today are the most similar to those used by the United Provinces of Central America. The triangle, volcanoes, rising sun, Cap of Liberty, and rainbow all appeared on the original emblem. The coat of arms used today contains the name of the state, *Republica de*

Nicaragua, whereas in 1823, the title was *Provincias Unidas del Centro de America*.

In 1908 the decision to revert to the emblems which are used by the United Provinces of Central America was made to reflect Nicaragua's aspirations for the rebirth of the political entity formed by the five nations.

ARMS OF NICARAGUA

The rays of the sun and the rainbow are symbolic of the bright future

The Cap of Liberty represents national freedom

The five volcanoes represent the original five member states

Costa Rica

Adopted November 27, 1848 | **Ratio** 3:5 | **Usage** National and State

Blue and white were the colors of the original flag of the United Provinces of Central America

Red, white, and blue recall the colors of the French *Tricolore*

Costa Rica was a signatory to the Declaration of Independence from Spain in 1821, joining the United Provinces of Central America (1823–38).

The Central American flag remained in use in Costa Rica until 1848 when, in response to events in France, it was decided to incorporate the French colors into the national flag. This was done by adding a central red stripe. The coat of arms was also revised and placed in the center of the flag. In 1906, it was placed in a white disk on the red stripe, and later on an oval, set toward the hoist.

The coat of arms depicts the isthmus between the Pacific Ocean and the Caribbean Sea. The stars stand for the seven provinces and the Central American union is recalled by "*America Central*" on the upper scroll.

ARMS OF COSTA RICA

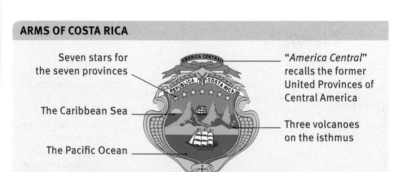

Seven stars for the seven provinces

The Caribbean Sea

The Pacific Ocean

"*America Central*" recalls the former United Provinces of Central America

Three volcanoes on the isthmus

Panama

Adopted November 3, 1903 | **Ratio** 2:3 | **Usage** National and Civil

Blue was the color of the Conservatives and red that of the Liberals

Although inspired by the Stars and Stripes, the stars and quarters are said to represent the two main political parties

White symbolizes peace in the country

Panama, originally a province of Colombia, was detached in 1903 to secure the building of the Panama Canal within a US-controlled zone.

The first flag, proposed back in 1903, consisted of seven horizontal stripes of red and yellow, with a blue canton containing two golden suns, joined by a narrow line to depict the oceans to be united by the Panama Canal.

However, this was not accepted by the Panamanian leader, Manuel Amador Guerrero, whose family designed a new flag. Although clearly modeled on the US flag, the stars and quarters are said to stand for the rival political parties, and the white for the peace in which they operate.

The coat of arms reflects Panama's transition from civil war to peace in 1903, and the increased prosperity this promised the people.

ARMS OF PANAMA

The shield depicts tools, weapons, a cornucopia, and a winged wheel, which together symbolize a move from war, to peace and prosperity

The national motto— "*Pro Mundi Beneficio*," meaning "For the Benefit of the World"

The northern and southern hemispheres joined by the Panama Canal

Jamaica

Adopted August 6, 1962 | **Ratio** 1:2 | **Usage** National and Civil

Black, green, and gold are also Pan-African colors

"Hardships there are but the land is green and the sun shineth" is the local motto complementing the flag

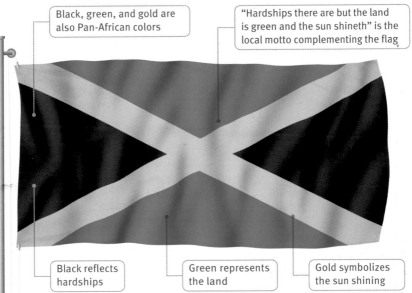

Black reflects hardships

Green represents the land

Gold symbolizes the sun shining

Jamaica was a British colony from 1655 until 1962. From 1958 onward, it was part of the West Indies Federation, which was dissolved in 1962.

The present design emerged from those sent in by the public in a national competition. It was originally designed with horizontal stripes, but this was too similar to the then Tanganyikan flag, and as a result, the saltire was substituted.

The coat of arms, based on those granted to Jamaica on February 3, 1663, is among the oldest granted to a British colony. It was used on the former British flags of Jamaica.

THE QUEEN'S STANDARD

The flag for HM Queen Elizabeth II, was introduced after independence. It contains a banner of the arms, with the Queen's Cypher in the center. The field depicts the red Cross of St. George charged with pineapples.

BANNER OF THE QUEEN OF JAMAICA

The Royal Cypher is enclosed within a chaplet of roses

St. George's Cross

The four pineapples and cross are taken from the Arms of Jamaica

Cuba

Adopted June 25, 1848 | **Ratio** 1:2 | **Usage** National and Civil

The triangle comes from the Masonic symbol for equality

The design is based on the US Stars and Stripes

"La Estrella Solitaria"— the Lone Star

Cuba, the only communist state in the Americas, was a Spanish colony until 1898, when it was ceded to the US. It gained independence in 1902.

The flag was designed in 1848 for the liberation movement, which sought to detach Cuba from Spain and make it into a state of the US. The "Lone Star" represented another star which would be added to "the splendid North American constellation."

The triangle is derived from the Masonic symbol for equality, while the five stripes stand for the five provinces of the time. The flag was briefly hoisted in 1850 at Cardenas, but was not officially adopted until 1902, when independence was granted by the US.

Another flag from the 19th century is that of Carlos Manuel de Céspedes, used by the independence movement of 1868–78. It is now used as the Jack of the Cuban navy.

FLAG OF CÉSPEDES

The flag is like that of Chile with the blue and red reversed

This flag was also modeled on the Stars and Stripes, using the same colors: blue, red, and white, and a star in the canton

Bahamas

Adopted July 10, 1973 | **Ratio** 1:2 | **Usage** National

Black represents the strength of the people

Blue recalls the Caribbean Sea

Yellow reflects the islands' sandy beaches

Originally a pirate base, the Bahamas became a formal British colony in 1783. It did not achieve independence until July 10, 1973.

The colors of the flag are intended to represent the aquamarine waters surrounding the islands and their golden sandy beaches. The flag is based on designs by the Bahamian people. Many of those submitted also included the idea of sunrise, which has been incorporated into the coat of arms.

The Bahamas Civil Ensign (flown by merchant ships) is often seen, since many ships are registered in the Bahamas. The flag is based on the British Red Ensign—red with a Bahamian national flag in the canton—but is distinguished by the white cross, like the Cross of St. George, across the red field.

The Bahamas has many other flags including one for the specific use of the prime minister.

BAHAMAS CIVIL ENSIGN

The national flag is placed in the canton

The civil ensign is distinguished from government and naval ensigns by its red field

Haiti

Adopted February 17, 1986 | **Ratio** 3:5 | **Usage** National and State

Blue and red are taken from the French *Tricolore*

Haiti became a French colony in 1697, but in 1803 a rebellion broke out. Independence was granted on January 1, 1804.

The blue and red of the flag were retained after a French *Tricolore* was torn up by the rebel Jean-Jacques Dessalines in 1803. The two parts were stitched together horizontally to make a new flag.

However, a rival flag of vertical black and red panels was also used at various times, most recently in the period from 1964–86, during the regime of the Duvalier family. Since 1843, the flag for official and state use has had the arms on a white panel in the center. The coat of arms depicts a trophy of weapons ready to defend freedom, and a royal palm topped with a Cap of Liberty for the country's independence.

ARMS OF HAITI

The Cap of Liberty

The royal palm symbolizes independence

The national motto—
"*L'Union Fait La Force*," meaning "Union is Strength"

Weapons reflect the people's willingness to defend their liberty

Dominican Republic

Adopted November 6, 1844 | **Ratio** 2:3 | **Usage** National and State

Blue and red are taken from the flag of Haiti, which once controlled the Dominican Republic

The coat of arms only appears on the flag for national and state use

The cross of the Trinitarian independence movement

A Spanish colony, briefly occupied by Haiti (1820–44), the Trinitarian movement was formed to free the country. Dominican Republic was liberated in 1844.

The flag was designed by the leader of the Trinitarians, Juan Pablo Duarte. He altered the layout of the blue and red of the Haitian flag, placing a large white cross over it to symbolize faith.

A DISTINCTIVE NATIONAL FLAG
To create distinct flags for state and civil use, the coat of arms, adopted in 1844, was placed on the state flag. The civil flag, on both land and sea, does not carry the arms.

The arms depicts a Bible open at the first chapter of St. John's Gospel. This is placed on a trophy of national flags, on a shield of the same design. The Trinitarian motto is above this and the name of the state below.

ARMS OF DOMINICAN REPUBLIC

Gospel of St. John, a Trinitarian emblem

The password of the Trinitarian movement— *"Dios, Patria, Libertad"* ("God, Country, Freedom")

The lower scroll contains the state title

St. Kitts & Nevis

Adopted September 19, 1983 | **Ratio** 2:3 | **Usage** National and Civil

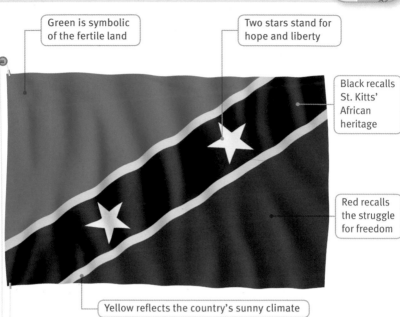

Green is symbolic of the fertile land

Two stars stand for hope and liberty

Black recalls St. Kitts' African heritage

Red recalls the struggle for freedom

Yellow reflects the country's sunny climate

A British colony in the Leeward Islands since 1873, the islands of St. Kitts and Nevis gained independence together in 1983.

The flag was the winning entry in a local competition which attracted 258 entries, and was the work of a student, Edrice Lewis. It was she who gave what is now the official interpretation of the flag—that its colors stand for the fertile land, year-round sunshine, the struggle for freedom, and the African heritage. The two stars stand for hope and liberty, not for the islands of St. Kitts and Nevis.

THE FLAG OF NEVIS

The island of Nevis has a flag of its own, which is bright yellow, with a stylized image of Nevis Peak. The national flag is in the canton. St. Kitts also has an ensign for the Coast Guard.

THE FLAG OF NEVIS

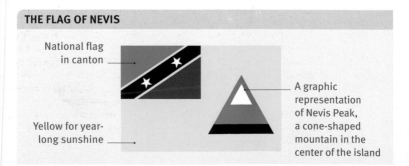

National flag in canton

A graphic representation of Nevis Peak, a cone-shaped mountain in the center of the island

Yellow for year-long sunshine

Antigua & Barbuda

Adopted February 27, 1967 | **Ratio** 2:3 | **Usage** National and Civil

Black recalls the islands' African heritage

The rising sun represents a new era

White symbolizes hope

Blue represents the Caribbean Sea

From 1632 until formal independence was granted in 1981, Antigua and its neighbor Barbuda were British colonies.

The flag dates from the inception of self-government in 1967 and was the winning design in a competition which more than 600 local people entered.

THE SYMBOLISM OF THE FLAG
The designer, Reginald Samuel, interpreted it as representing the sun rising against the background of the peoples' African heritage in a new era. The overall V-shape stands for victory. It is on a red background, which symbolizes the dynamism of the population. Blue is for the sea, and white is for hope.

THE NEW NATIONAL FLAG
The flag was retained unchanged when Antigua became independent.

Barbuda does not have a separate flag, although there is one for Redonda, an uninhabited island whose "throne" is claimed by several rival "monarchs."

THE NATIONAL ARMS
The coat of arms was granted in 1977 and depicts a shield with a sugar mill, once the primary industry, on a background of white and blue waves. Above this is a sun on a black background. The shield stands on a sea island. The crest is a pineapple from the arms of the former colony of the Leeward Islands, of which Antigua was once a part. Beneath is a scroll with the national motto: "Each endeavoring, all achieving."

Dominica

Adopted November 3, 1978 | **Ratio** 1:2 | **Usage** National and Civil

Yellow recalls the original inhabitants

The stars represent the ten parishes

White symbolizes the region's pure water

Black is for the fertile soil

The sisserou parrot is unique to Dominica

First colonized by the French, Dominica came under British control in 1759. It became a British Associated State in 1967 and independent in 1978.

The flag adopted in 1978 features the national bird emblem, the sisserou parrot, which also appears on the coat of arms granted on July 21, 1961. This parrot can only be found in Dominica. It is an endangered species; only a few pairs remain.

The green field represents the lush vegetation of the island. The cross represents the Trinity and the Christian faith: its three colors recall the native Indians, the fertile soil, and the pure water. The ten stars stand for the ten parishes and the red disk for social justice.

The flag of the president has a dark green field with the coat of arms in the center, crowned with a British lion. It depicts palm trees, an indigenous frog, and the sea.

THE PRESIDENT'S FLAG

The national motto is in Creole—"*Aprés Bondie C'est La Ter*," meaning "After the good Lord (we love) the soil"

Two sisserou parrots support the coat of arms

St. Lucia

Adopted March 1, 1967 | **Ratio** 1:2 | **Usage** National and Civil

The blue field represents the sea

This symbol represents twin peaks of the Pitons—famous volcanic mountains

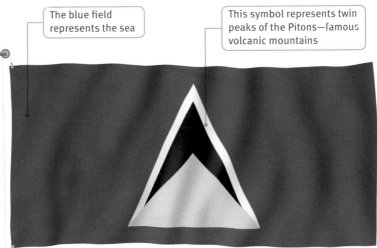

St. Lucia, first settled in 1605, was fought over by the French and the British, finally being ceded to Britain in 1814. It became independent in 1979.

The flag was adopted when St. Lucia became a British Associated State in 1967. It was designed by a local artist, Dunstan St. Omer. The blue field represents the sea, from which arise the twin peaks of the Pitons said to be "rising sheer out of the sea and looking skyward—a symbol of hope." The yellow triangle stands for sunshine, and the black arrowhead on white, for the twin cultures of the island. After gaining independence, the flag was retained, but the height of the yellow triangle was increased.

A new form of the arms was also adopted, symbolizing the national motto: "The Land, the People, the Light." Apart from the governor-general's flag and that of the capital, Castries, no other flags are known.

THE GOVERNOR-GENERAL'S STANDARD

The state's title is placed on the scroll

The British Royal Crest of a crowned lion standing on a St. Edward's Crown

St. Vincent & the Grenadines

Adopted October 12, 1985 | **Ratio** 2:3 | **Usage** National and Civil

Blue recalls the sky

Yellow represents the sunshine

Green represents the islands' abundant vegetation

Diamond shapes represent "Gems of the Antilles"

St. Vincent was occupied by the British in 1762. It achieved independence in 1979, together with the Grenadines, a chain of adjacent islands.

The basic design and colors of the flag date from the flag hoisted on the day of independence in 1979. It had the arms of the islands placed on a stylized breadfruit leaf in the center. Its blue, yellow, and green stripes were derived from the common colors of the flags assigned to the Associated States by the College of Arms. The breadfruit recalled the British introduction of the breadfruit tree into the Caribbean from the South Seas in the late 18th Century.

Although this first flag was designed by a local islander, the design did not meet the approval of all the people of St. Vincent and the Grenadines, and, in 1985, moves were made to secure a new design.

A NEW NATIONAL FLAG

After a local competition failed to produce a satisfactory design, the problem was submitted to a Swiss graphic artist who suggested what is now the current design. In this, the "V" formed by the diamonds stands for St. Vincent, and the diamonds represent its local sobriquet the "Gems of the Antilles."

ARMS OF ST. VINCENT

The coat of arms was first introduced in 1912. It depicts two women, one standing holding an olive branch, the other kneeling to represent peace and justice, which is also the national motto—"*Pax, Justitia*." This appears on a scroll at the base.

Barbados

Adopted November 30, 1966 | **Ratio** 2:3 | **Usage** National and Civil

Blue represents the sea

The trident broken from its shaft represents a break with the past

Gold reflects the golden sands of Barbados

Barbados was first settled by the British in 1627. It became a colony and achieved self-government in 1961 and independence in 1966.

The current flag was adopted at the time of independence. It was the winning design in a national competition, which was won by Grantley Prescod, a local art teacher.

THE SYMBOLISM OF THE FLAG

Prescod interpreted the stripes as representing the blue seas and the golden sands which surround the island. The trident is adapted from the previous flag badge which depicted Britannia holding a trident (symbolic of her rule over the seas). Here the trident is without a shaft, indicating a break with its colonial past. It is also the emblem of the sea god, Neptune, and reflects the importance of the sea to Barbados.

ARMS OF BARBADOS

The coat of arms was granted by HM Queen Elizabeth II in 1966, on a visit to the island. The shield depicts a bearded fig tree, after which the island takes its name, between two "Pride of Barbados" flowers. The crest is an arm holding two sugarcanes in the form of a St. Andrew's Cross. This commemorates independence, which was achieved on St. Andrew's Day, November 30, in 1966.

Barbados also has a Governor's standard. It is the same as that of the Governor of St. Lucia, which features the Royal Crest of England with a British lion (see p.73), except that it bears the title "Barbados" on the scroll beneath the Royal Crest.

Grenada

Adopted February 7, 1974 | **Ratio** 3:5 | **Usage** National and Civil

A nutmeg, which is Grenada's most famous product

The central star and disk represent the capital St. George's

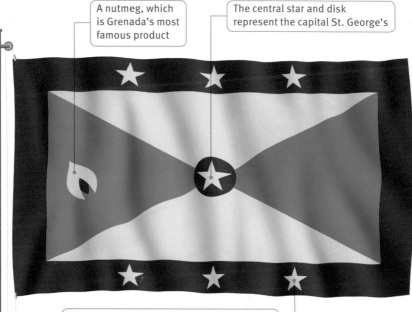

The six outer stars stand for the six parishes

First settled by France, Grenada was invaded by Britain in 1762. It became an Associated State in 1967 and fully independent in 1974.

The flag used prior to independence in 1967 also featured a nutmeg, since Grenada is a major world supplier of this commodity, and is known as the "Spice Island."

Other features of the flag derive from the coat of arms granted on December 6, 1973, including the red, yellow, and green colors.

SYMBOLISM OF THE FLAG

The yellow star on a red disc stands for the Borough of St. George's, Grenada's capital, and the other six stars for the remaining six parishes.

In the official interpretation the red stands for courage and vitality, the yellow for wisdom and warmth, and the green for vegetation and agriculture.

When the flag is used at sea its proportions are altered from 3:5 to a longer form (1:2).

THE NATIONAL ARMS

The coat of arms depicts the Santa Maria, Columbus' ship, a lion representing national liberty, and a lily emblem symbolizing the Virgin Mary. The shield is supported by two characteristic local creatures, an armadillo and a ramier pigeon. Beneath the shield is a representation of the Grand Etang lake, and, on a scroll at the base, what must be one of the world's longest national mottos: "Ever conscious of God we aspire, build and advance as one people."

Trinidad & Tobago

Adopted August 31, 1962 | **Ratio** 3:5 | **Usage** National and Civil

White represents the sea

Black symbolizes the strength of the people

Red stands for the people

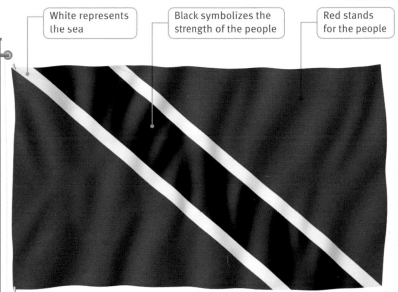

Trinidad and Tobago were separate British colonies, which united in 1889. They became independent in 1962 and a republic in 1976.

The flag adopted at independence was chosen from among designs sent in by the public. The same colors are used in the arms.

A flag for HM Queen Elizabeth II was adopted after independence, but it became obsolete following the formation of the republic.

The President has a flag of blue with the coat of arms in the center. It depicts the three ships of Columbus who landed here in 1498. Above the ships are two golden hummingbirds. The supporters of the coat of arms are also local birds and the whole shield stands on a scene depicting waves breaking against the rocky coasts of the islands.

Trinidad also has flags for the Prime Minister and other ministers.

THE PRESIDENT'S FLAG

The scarlet ibis is one of many local birds

The top of the shield depicts two hummingbirds

The *cocrico* – a local bird

In 1498, Columbus discovered Trinidad and his ships appear on the shield

South America

Colombia

Adopted December 17, 1819 | **Ratio** 2:3 | **Usage** National

The colors are those of Francisco de Miranda, the liberation leader

The original yellow band was doubled in width when Greater Colombia was formed

Yellow recalls the federation of Greater Colombia

Blue represents independence from Spain

Red represents courage

Following years of Spanish rule, Colombia became part of independent Greater Colombia in 1819, and then a separate republic in 1830.

The flag of Greater Colombia, adopted in 1819, was retained by Colombia after independence in 1830. For a while the stripes were arranged vertically, but the original version was restored in 1861.

There are two variant flags. The civil ensign has a red-bordered, blue oval bearing a white star in the center, used to distinguish it from the flag of Ecuador. The state flag and naval ensign have the arms in the center.

THE NATIONAL ARMS
The coat of arms dates from 1834. It includes a pomegranate, the symbol of Granada in Spain, after which the area was once named.

ARMS OF COLOMBIA

National motto—
Libertad y Orden, meaning "Liberty and Order"

The Cap of Liberty

A map of the Isthmus of Panama

The crest is a condor, frequently used in South American heraldry

A pomegranate recalls New Granada, Colombia's former name when a Spanish colony

Venezuela

Adopted March 12, 2006 | **Ratio** 2:3 | **Usage** National and Civil

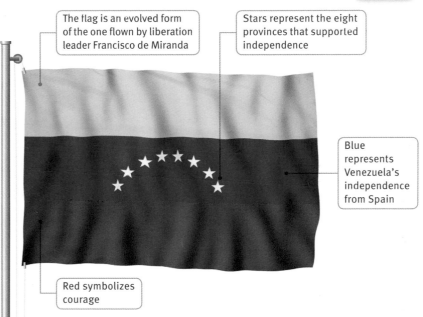

The flag is an evolved form of the one flown by liberation leader Francisco de Miranda

Stars represent the eight provinces that supported independence

Blue represents Venezuela's independence from Spain

Red symbolizes courage

Venezuela was once part of the Spanish province of New Granada. It then joined Greater Colombia from 1819 until independence in 1830.

The Venezuelan flag was the invention of Francisco de Miranda, who initiated the freedom of New Granada in 1806. At that time it had no stars; they were added in 1836 to symbolize the provinces that had supported the Declaration of Independence in 1811. The original plain tricolor was altered in 1819, making the yellow double width, for use as the flag of Greater Colombia.

After independence in 1836, the flag reverted to stripes of equal width and the stars were added. The coat of arms dates from the 19th century but has altered frequently, especially the inscription. The present form dates from 2006.

ARMS OF VENEZUELA

The wheatsheaf represents fertility

A galloping horse symbolizes liberty

The name of the state, *Republica Bolivariana de Venezuela*

Two horns of plenty symbolize abundance

The flag and weapons represent independence and the early native people

The arms appear in the canton of the state flag and naval ensign

Guyana

Adopted May 26, 1966 | **Ratio** 3:5 | **Usage** National and Civil

Red recalls the people's dynamism and zeal for reform

The "Golden Arrow" represents a bright future

Green recalls the vast forests and fields

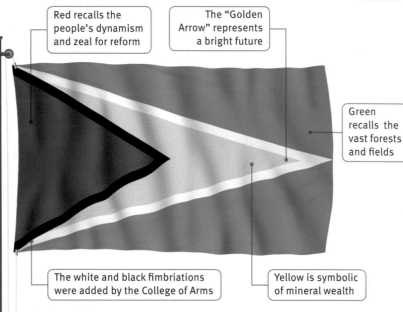

The white and black fimbriations were added by the College of Arms

Yellow is symbolic of mineral wealth

Guyana was acquired by the UK in 1814. It became independent in 1966 and a republic within the Commonwealth in 1970.

The flag is known as the "Golden Arrow" because of the arrowhead that flies across the green field. The College of Arms altered the original design's red field in 1966 and also added the black and white fimbriations. The green and yellow represent natural resources and the red "zeal and dynamism [of the inhabitants] in building the nation."

GUYANA'S ARMS
Guyana's arms includes a headdress symbolizing its indigenous population, and is supported by two jaguars holding items representing its mining industry. The national motto, "One people, One Nation, One Destiny," appears on the scroll below the shield.

STANDARD OF GUYANA

Amerindian head-dress symbolizes the indigenous people of the country

A shield decorated with the national flower (*Victoria Regia* Lily)

A *Victoria Regia* water lily, growing from stylized heraldic water

Wavy lines represent the waters of Guyana; below is the Canje Pheasant

Suriname

Adopted November 25, 1975 | **Ratio** 2:3 | **Usage** National and Civil

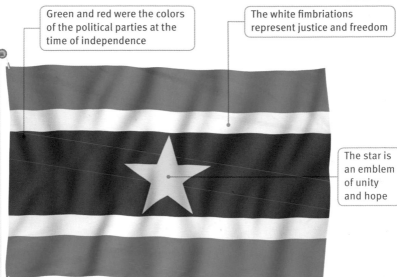

Green and red were the colors of the political parties at the time of independence

The white fimbriations represent justice and freedom

The star is an emblem of unity and hope

Suriname was part of the Dutch kingdom until 1975. Since independence, there have been a series of coups and changes of constitution.

The flag was chosen in 1975 by a parliamentary commission, based on designs sent in by the public. The goal was to choose a flag which harmonized the colors of the main political groups (green and red) into a design suggestive of unity and progress. The star is thus the emblem of unity and hope for the future, and the white fimbriations, separating the red and green, stand for justice and freedom.

THE PRESIDENT'S STANDARD
This has a white panel in place of the star and contains the state arms. The coat of arms dates back to the 17th century and the time of Dutch rule, but was revised in 1959 and again in 1975.

THE PRESIDENT'S STANDARD

On the shield, a ship reflects commerce, a diamond, mining, and a tree, agriculture

The supporters are Native Americans

The national motto—"*Justitia, Pietas, Fides*" meaning "Justice, Peace, Faith"

Ecuador

Adopted September 26, 1860 | **Ratio** 1:2 | **Usage** National

Yellow, blue, and red are the colors of Venezuelan revolutionary Francisco de Miranda

Yellow symbolizes the crops and fertile soil

Red symbolizes courage

Blue recalls independence from Spain

Ecuador, formerly a Spanish colony, joined the state of Greater Colombia in 1822. It seceded from the federation in 1830 to form a republic.

The 1819 flag of Greater Colombia was restored in Ecuador in 1860, and since then the flags of Ecuador and Colombia have been very similar. The national arms were added to the center of the basic civil flag in 1900, creating a distinct flag for national and state purposes. The civil flag on land and at sea does not contain the arms, making it almost identical to the flag of Colombia, except for its proportions. When used abroad, the flag always contains the arms.

ARMS OF ECUADOR

The coat of arms dates from 1845 and depicts Mount Chimborazo and the mouth of the Guyas River.

ARMS OF ECUADOR

Four signs of the zodiac represent the months from March to May

An allegorical scene depicts Mount Chimborazo, South America's highest peak

An Andean condor symbolizes bravery and liberty

A ship at the mouth of the Guyas River representing commerce

The ax and fasces are symbols of republicanism

Peru

Adopted February 25, 1825 | **Ratio** 2:3 | **Usage** National

Red and white are the colors chosen by San Martín, *El Liberador* ("the Liberator")

The colors also recall those of the Incas, who ruled much of Peru until European colonization

Peru was freed from Spanish rule in 1819 by an army led by José de San Martín. Since 1824 it has been an independent unitary republic.

The colors chosen by San Martín for the Peruvian Legion were red and white, said to be the colors of the Inca Empire, and the rising sun, also dating back to the Incas. The flag assumed its present form, dropping the sun in 1825, at the behest of Simón Bolívar, another famous liberator. As is usual in former Spanish colonies, the official flag, used by the government and the armed forces, has the coat of arms in the center.

The coat of arms dates from 1825 and depicts a cornucopia, a *cinchona* tree, and a *vicuña*, surrounded by state flags. The flags do not appear on the arms placed on the official flag.

ARMS OF PERU

A *vicuña*, the national animal of Peru

On the coat of arms, the wreaths are substituted for national flags

Cinchona, the source of quinine

A cornucopia symbolizing prosperity

Brazil

Adopted November 15, 1889 | **Ratio** 7:10 | **Usage** National and Civil

Green recalls the Brazilian rain forest

The national motto meaning "Order and Progress," is on the band

Yellow represents the country's mineral resources

The most recent stars were added to the *Canis Major* constellation

Each star represents a state in the Federation

Brazil belonged to Portugal until 1822 when it became an independent kingdom, and later an empire. It formed a federal republic in 1889.

The green field and yellow lozenge were part of the flag adopted in 1822 when independence was first achieved and the empire was declared. In 1889, the imperial arms were replaced by a view of the night sky as it appeared over Rio de Janeiro when the republic was formed. Each of the stars in the constellation represents a state of the Federation, including the Federal District. These have been altered from time to time, most recently in 1992 when the number of stars increased to 27.

THE CONSTELLATIONS

The constellations on Brazil's flag are represented in a realistic manner, with stars of varying sizes, although the size of star does not reflect the importance of the state. In 1992, new stars were added to the constellation of *Canis Major* in the lower left section of the sky. The country's national motto, "*Ordem e Progresso*," meaning "Order and Progress," appears on a band across the center of the night sky.

THE NATIONAL CAPITAL

In Brasília, the capital city since 1960, stands one of the world's tallest flagpoles, on which flies an enormous national flag.

Brazil also has flags for the president, the Ministry of Marine, and a naval Jack.

Brazil: State flags

Many of the flags recall historical events or the formation of the federal republic. The date of accession is next to the state name.

The Federal District 1960

The flag of the Federal District dates from 1969. The green rectangle contains four arrows representing the balance of centralization and devolution in Brazil.

Acre 1962

Adopted by the republic declared in 1899, when Acre was still part of Bolivia, the flag was retained by the state and the star was added to recall its joining the Federation.

Alagoas 1889

Based on the flag of 1894, this new version was instituted in 1963. In the center is the arms, also originally dating back to 1894. It recalls various aspects of the state's industry.

Amapá 1989

The flag was adopted in 1984 for the territory and retained for the state. It uses all the national colors, together with an outline of the fortress of Macapá, the state capital.

State flags (continued)

Amazonas 1889

The flag dates from the local uprising of 1897. The stars stand for the 25 municipalities, with the large one for Manaus, the state capital. The flag was regularized in 1982.

Bahia 1889

The flag dates back to the uprisings of 1789 and 1798, which are recalled by the white triangle. The flag in this form was first adopted in 1889, when Bahia joined the Federation.

Ceará 1889

The flag was instituted in 1922 and is very similar to the national flag. The arms depicts an allegorical landscape surrounded by stars. It dates from 1897 and was revised in 1967.

Espírito Santo 1889

The flag was created in 1947. The Portuguese motto meaning—"Work and Trust"—is from a Jesuit writer, and the pink and blue represent the local evening sky.

Goiás 1889

The flag is based on those promoted for the republic in 1889. This version has five stars for the Southern Cross similar to those in the national arms.

Maranhão 1889

The flag, adopted in 1889, features a star, which represents the state on the national flag, while the stripes stand for its ethnic mix.

Mato Grosso 1889

The flag is based on the national flag, but with local interpretations of the color arrangement and one star for the state. It was adopted in 1890.

Mato Grosso do Sul 1977

The design emerged from a competition held in 1978 after the new state was formed. The flag was instituted in 1979.

State flags (continued)

Minas Gerais 1889

The flag contains a Masonic triangle of the *Inconfidência Mineira* (miners' revolt) of 1789, standing for equality.

Pará 1889

Based on a republican flag, it dates from 1898. The star is taken from the one for Pará on the national flag.

Paraíba 1889

The flag recalls Vargas' revolution in 1930. *Nego* ("I deny it") refers to the assassination of the state president.

Paraná 1889

The flag contains an emblem like the national flag, bearing the Southern Cross and name of the state.

Pernambuco 1889

This is the flag of the Pernambuco revolution of 1817, which later became the flag of the state when the events of 1817 were celebrated.

Piauí 1889

Based on the colors of the national
flag, in this instance it only has one
star representing the state of Piauí.
It was adopted in 1922.

Rio de Janeiro 1975

The state was reconstituted in 1975
to include the state of Guanabara.
The new state took over the emblems
of the former solo state of Rio de Janeiro.

Rio Grande do Norte 1889

Although it uses arms granted in 1909,
the flag only dates from 1957, thus
making it one of the newest flags of
the original states.

Rio Grande do Sul 1889

The flag dates from the revolution of 1836,
which created the Republic of Rio Grande
do Sul. It was readopted in 1889; the arms
were added in 1891.

Rondônia 1981

Rondônia's flag uses the four national
colors and a single star symbol.
It was adopted in 1981 after a
design competition.

State flags (continued)

Roraima 1989

The flag, adopted when the territory became a federal state, uses the national colors and star, with a red line representing the Equator.

Santa Catarina 1889

The red and white flag precedes the republic. It was most recently regularized in 1953 when the arms were placed in the center.

São Paulo 1889

The flag was created in 1888 at the start of the republican revolution, and revived in 1932 with 13 stripes.

Sergipe 1889

The flag was created in the late 19th century and adopted in 1920. In 1951, the stars were repositioned.

Tocantins 1989

After achieving statehood, a flag and arms were adopted, using the national colors of blue and white.

Chile

Adopted October 18, 1817 | **Ratio** 2:3 | **Usage** National and Civil

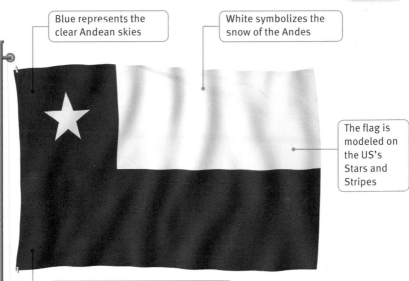

Blue represents the clear Andean skies

White symbolizes the snow of the Andes

The flag is modeled on the US's Stars and Stripes

Red is for the blood shed for freedom

Chile was freed from Spanish rule in 1818, largely through the efforts of José de San Martín, leader of the Army of the Andes.

Adopted in 1817 after San Martín's victory at Chacabuco, the national flag of Chile was preceded by at least two other versions during the early years of separatism. The current flag was based on the Stars and Stripes.

The white star was reserved for use exclusively on the official flag until 1864, when the starred flag was made official for all purposes.

THE PRESIDENT'S STANDARD
The flag of the president is the same as the national flag, with the national arms in the center. The coat of arms dates from 1834. It is supported by an huemal deer and a condor. The crest is formed from the feathers of the rhea bird. The motto—"*Por La Razon o La Fuerza*"—means "By reason or by force."

THE PRESIDENT'S STANDARD

An *huemal* deer, of the high Andes

A crest of feathers from the *rhea* bird

The condor is a common symbol on South American arms

Bolivia

Adopted November 30, 1851 | **Ratio** 15:22 | **Usage** National and Civil

The order of the stripes was changed to red, yellow, green in 1851; red and green were retained from the flag of 1825

Red recalls valor

Yellow reflects Bolivia's mineral reserves

Green symbolizes fertility

Bolivia, originally known as Upper Peru, was named after Simón Bolívar who supervised its secession from Spain in 1825.

The flag of 1825 had three stripes of green-red-green, with five gold stars within laurel wreaths. These stood for the original five departments.

A NEW TRICOLOR

In 1826, the flag was altered to three equal stripes of yellow, green and red with the arms in the center. It was last altered in 1851, when the order of the stripes was changed to red, yellow, green.

The official flag still has the arms in the center. It was regulated in 1888 and features a stylized scene containing Mount Potosí, an alpaca, a wheatsheaf, and a breadfruit tree.

ARMS OF BOLIVIA

The weapons and flags represent the people's willingness to defend the state

As on many South American arms, the crest is a condor

The allegorical scene on the shield represents Bolivia's agricultural and industrial wealth

The nine stars represent Bolivia's nine departments

Paraguay

Adopted November 25, 1842 | **Ratio** 3:5 | **Usage** National and Civil

The red, white, and blue colors were influenced by the French *Tricolore*, which had become a symbol of liberation

On the reverse, the flag is charged with the Treasury Seal

The Star of May is used as a symbol of freedom on many South American flags

Paraguay declared its independence from Spain in 1811 and has remained an independent republic ever since.

The colors of the flag and the Star of May emblem date from the Declaration of Independence. A number of variant designs existed prior to the current design, which was regularized in 1842. The current flag has a separate emblem on each side, a practice dating from the time of José de Francia, in power from 1814–40. During his regime one side of the flag carried the arms of Spain and the other the arms of Asunción.

The current emblems, adopted in 1821, but not officially sanctioned until 1842, are the national arms on the front (obverse) and the Treasury Seal on the back (reverse).

STATE ARMS ON THE OBVERSE

The Star of May recalls the date of independence

Name of the state

TREASURY SEAL ON THE REVERSE

The Cap of Liberty guarded by a lion

The motto, *"Paz y Justicia"* ("Peace and Justice")

Uruguay

Adopted July 11, 1830 | **Ratio** 2:3 | **Usage** National and Civil

The Sun of May has been a national emblem since the 19th century

White and blue are also the national colors of Argentina, from which this flag derives

The nine stripes represent the nine departments

Historically a Spanish colony, Uruguay was annexed to Brazil and then to Argentina before becoming fully independent in 1830.

The colors, blue and white, and the Sun of May on the current flag come from the Argentinian flag.

THE FLAG OF ARTIGAS

The colors were brought to Uruguay by José Artigas, who led the movement for separation. His flag was blue-and-white striped, with a red diagonal. Variations of this flag remained in use after Uruguay was annexed to Brazil in 1821.

When full independence was assumed, the present form of the flag was instituted. The nine stripes represent the nine departments. The Sun of May has been used as the national emblem since 1815 and now appears as the crest on the coat of arms.

FLAG OF ARTIGAS

This flag was used as a Jack for naval vessels until the late 1990s. The colors derive from those of Argentina's flag

Red represents the "*Banda Oriental*" (the "East Bank") of Uruguay

Argentina

Adopted February 27, 1812 | **Ratio** 9:14 | **Usage** National and Civil

Sky blue and white were formed into a flag by Manuel Belgrano, the leader of the revolution

Light blue and white are from the cockades used by revolutionaries in 1812

The sun was added in 1818 to create a flag for state use

Liberation demonstrations began in Buenos Aires on May 25, 1810. Argentina achieved its independence from Spain in 1816.

At his encampment at Rosario in 1812, the revolutionary commander, Manuel Belgrano needed a flag. He devised one, using the sky blue and white colors of the cockades worn by supporters of independence. This flag was used in battle and although initially rejected by the provisional government, it later became the national flag.

THE SUN FLAG

In 1818, the sun emblem was added to the national flag, forming the state flag flown on government buildings and military bases. It is also the Argentine naval ensign. The sun is based on coins issued in Buenos Aires in 1813. The tradition of the "Sun of May," breaking through white clouds in a blue sky has no historical basis.

ARMS OF ARGENTINA

The Cap of Liberty

The sun symbolizes the dawn of a new era and a new nation

Sky blue and white are the national colors

A wreath of laurels

Africa

Morocco

Adopted November 17, 1915 | **Ratio** 2:3 | **Usage** National and Civil

Red represents the descendants of the Prophet Muhammad

The Seal of Solomon was added in 1915

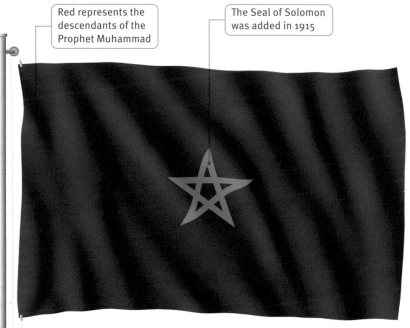

Morocco has been independent since 1956, becoming a kingdom in 1957. The state has occupied Western Sahara since 1975.

Red has considerable historic significance in Morocco, proclaiming the descent of the royal family from the Prophet Muhammad via Fatima, the wife of Ali, the fourth Caliph. Red is also the color that was used by the Sherifs of Mecca and the Imams of Yemen.

THE SEAL OF SOLOMON

Starting in the 17th century, when Morocco was ruled by the Hassani Dynasty, the flags of the country were plain red. In 1915, during the reign of Mulay Yusuf, the green "Seal of Solomon" was added to the national flag. The Seal is an interlaced pentangle, used as a symbol in occult law for centuries.

THE COLONIAL ERA

While Morocco was under French and Spanish control, the red flag with the Seal in the center remained in use but only inland; its use at sea was prohibited. When independence was restored in 1956 it once again became the national flag.

THE NATIONAL ARMS

After independence in 1958, Morocco adopted a national coat of arms. This depicts the sun rising over the Atlas Mountains. The arms also includes the Seal of Solomon from the national flag. On the scroll is an inscription from the Qur'an (Koran), which reads "If you assist God, he will assist you."

Algeria

Adopted July 3, 1962 | **Ratio** 2:3 | **Usage** National and Civil

Green is the color of Islam

The longer-than-usual horns stand for good fortune and happiness

White is symbolic of purity

Red represents liberty

The crescent and star of Islam recall Ottoman rule

Algeria was occupied by the French from 1830. Independence was achieved in 1962 after a long struggle led by the National Liberation Front.

The flag of Algeria was adopted by the National Liberation Front (*Front de Libération National*) in 1954, based on an older design, created in 1928, by the nationalist leader Messali Hadj. From 1958–62 it was the flag of the Provisional Government in exile, but it was retained when independence was achieved in 1962 and has remained unchanged ever since.

SYMBOLISM IN THE FLAG

The green in the hoist is the traditional color of Islam and the white represents purity. The horns of the crescent are longer than usual and represent increase or good fortune and happiness, while

the whole emblem recalls the period of Ottoman rule during the 16th century and its color, red, is symbolic of liberty.

THE NAVAL ENSIGN

The naval ensign has two crossed anchors in the canton. This device is used on the naval ensigns of several Arab countries, following the example of Egypt.

THE EMBLEM OF ALGERIA

The state coat of arms is based on the well-known local emblem of the "Hand of Fatima." It also contains the crescent and star of Islam, alongside symbols reflecting both agriculture and industry.

Tunisia

Adopted 1835 | **Ratio** 2:3 | **Usage** National and Civil

Red taken from the flag of Turkey

The crescent and star of Islam

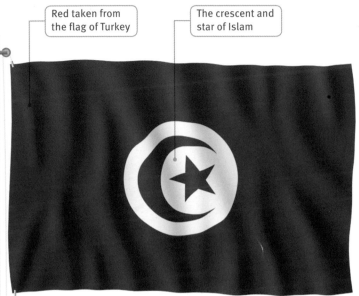

Tunisia was part of the Turkish Empire until 1881, when it became a French Protectorate. In 1957, it became a republic when the "Bey" was deposed.

The flag is based on that of the Turkish Empire and was adopted by the "Bey," the hereditary ruler of Tunisia, in 1835, primarily as a military flag. During the French administration (1881–1957) it became a sea flag, with the French *Tricolore* in the canton; this was removed when independence was achieved in 1956.

The coat of arms of Tunisia has been altered since the abolition of the monarchy, most recently in 1963, and unusually has the motto on a scroll actually on the shield. The motto reads—in Arabic—"Order, Liberty, Justice." The ship, lion, and balance were retained from the previous arms.

ARMS OF TUNISIA

The ship, lion, and balance symbolize the national motto

The ship also recalls early settlers

The national motto— "Order, Liberty, Justice"

Libya

Adopted August 3, 2011 | **Ratio** 1:2 | **Usage** National and Civil

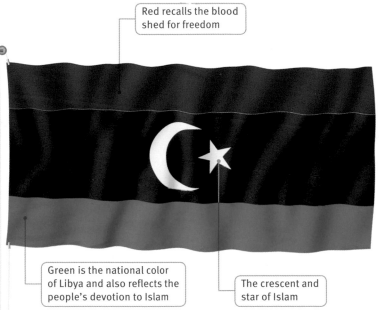

Red recalls the blood shed for freedom

Green is the national color of Libya and also reflects the people's devotion to Islam

The crescent and star of Islam

Libya achieved independence in 1951, but became a republic in 1967, led by Colonel Gaddafi. In 2011, the country held its first free election in 40 years.

The flag was designed by Omar Faiek Shennib after the creation of Libya in 1951. Following the revolution of 1969, the flag became three stripes of red, white, and black. In 1971, Libya joined the Federation of Arab Republics with Egypt and Syria, and adopted a flag with a hawk emblem in the center and the country's name beneath it. When Libya quit the Federation, Colonel Gaddafi chose a plain green flag—the only national flag without a design, insignia, or any other detail. The country reverted to its original flag during the Arab Spring uprising in 2011, when Gaddafi was ousted after 42 years. The new national seal bears a crescent moon and star, and the name of the new government.

NATIONAL FLAG OF LIBYA 1977-2011

Green symbolizes Gadaffi's political philosophy (after his *The Green Book*)

The absence of design made this the only national flag to be a single plain color

Egypt

Adopted October 4, 1984 | **Ratio** 2:3 | **Usage** National and Civil

Red, white, and black
are Pan-Arab colors

Eagle of Saladin

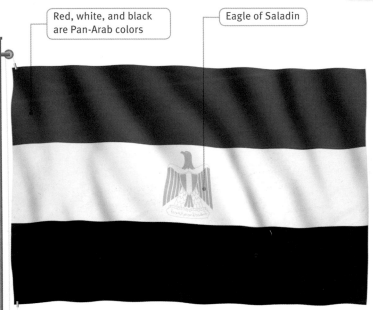

Egypt was a kingdom until 1953. Between 1958–61 it was part of the United Arab Republic (UAR), and from 1972–77, the Federation of Arab Republics.

As a kingdom, the flag was green with a white crescent and three stars.

THE UNITED ARAB REPUBLIC

When the United Arab Republic (UAR) was formed in 1958, they adapted the flag of the Liberation Rally, which led the independence revolt of 1952–53. The UAR flag was red, white, and black, with two green stars in the center of the white stripe. In 1972, when the Federation was formed, the stars were replaced with the Hawk of the Quraish, in gold, above the state name.

In 1984, Egypt reverted to the gold eagle used by the Liberation Rally. These colors and the eagle emblem have been widely copied in other Arab countries.

FLAG OF THE LIBERATION RALLY 1952–58

The gold eagle
is said to be the
Eagle of Saladin

The crescent
and stars were
retained from the
old national flag

Sudan

Adopted May 20, 1970 | **Ratio** 1:2 | **Usage** National and Civil

Red represents socialism

White represents purity and optimism

Green is the color of Islam and prosperity

Black is for the dark pre-Islamic past

Ruled jointly by Egypt and Britain from 1877, Sudan became independent in 1956. Since then it has had a series of different regimes.

The flag used at independence was a horizontal tricolor of blue, yellow, and green, but following the formation of the Democratic Republic in 1968, a new flag was chosen in a competition.

A PAN-ARAB FLAG

This design is like many other Arab flags. The green triangle at the hoist represents Islam and prosperity. White represents purity and optimism, red is for socialism, and black for the dark, pre-Islamic past.

In 1969 a new arms was adopted, with a secretary bird bearing a shield from the time of the Mahdi, (who briefly ruled Sudan in the 19th century). Two scrolls are placed above and below the bird.

ARMS OF SUDAN

The title of the state—
"*Al-Jamhuriya as-Sudaniya*"
("Republic of Sudan")

The national motto—
"*Al-nasr lina*"
("Victory is ours")

A secretary bird bears the shield

South Sudan

Adopted July 9, 2005 | **Ratio** 1:2 | **Usage** National and Civil

Blue represents the River Nile

Red recalls the martyrs of war

The star symbolizes people's unity in defending national freedom

South Sudan declared its independence from Sudan in 2011 following a national referendum that passed with almost 99 percent of the vote.

During their struggle with the rest of Sudan, the South Sudanese created a banner of independence that was used by the Sudan People's Liberation Movement. This eventually became the new national flag after the signing of a peace agreement that ended the civil war. The flag was officially hoisted when the country declared itself a sovereign state on July 9, 2005 (although full independence was achieved in 2011).

The flag is made up of six different colors: black, red, green, white, blue, and yellow. The black represents the country's population; the red recalls the blood that was shed during the war; the green symbolizes the country's natural resources and its verdant land; and the white represents the peace it has achieved after the struggle. The hoist side includes a yellow star upon a blue chevron. The blue recalls the River Nile, a source of life, while the star symbolizes the determination of its people in their endeavour to build a brighter future.

Before full independence, South Sudan had adoped a national emblem, which depicted a traditional African shield bearing the country's flag, crossed by lances, and supported by a shoebill and rhinoceros. However, this was replaced by a new national coat of arms, approved by the government in 2011. The new coat of arms consists of an African Kingfisher Eagle holding a scroll that bears the name of the state in English in its talons. The bird of prey embodies strength, resilience, and vision, while the shield and crossed spears represent the people's willingness to protect their new state and defend their liberty.

Eritrea

Adopted May 24, 1993 | **Ratio** 2:3 | **Usage** National and Civil

An olive branch is encircled by a wreath representing Eritrean autonomy

Green, blue, and red are the colors of the Eritrean People's Liberation Front

Eritrea was federated to Ethiopia in 1952 and fully integrated in 1962. From 1972, a long war of secession led to independence in 1993.

The flag of the Eritrean People's Liberation Front (ELPF), which campaigned for independence, is green and blue with a red triangle bearing a gold star. The flag adopted on gaining independence retained the colors and pattern, but replaced the star with the emblem used previously for autonomous Eritrea. This is an olive branch surrounded by a wreath of olive leaves. Originally this emblem was green on a blue flag, but it is now yellow.

THE PRESIDENT'S FLAG

The president's flag contains the national arms, which depicts a camel in a desert, with the name of the state underneath in English, Tigrinya, and Arabic.

THE PRESIDENT'S FLAG

The arms of Eritrea

The arms is surrounded by a wreath of leaves

The colors of the national flag are used

Djibouti

Adopted June 27, 1977 | **Ratio** 21:38 | **Usage** National and Civil

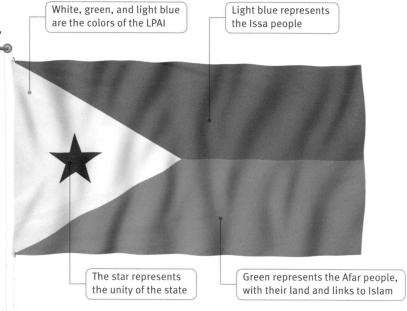

White, green, and light blue are the colors of the LPAI

Light blue represents the Issa people

The star represents the unity of the state

Green represents the Afar people, with their land and links to Islam

Once known as French Somaliland, and from 1967 as the Territory of the Afars and Issas, Djibouti gained independence in 1977.

The national flag adopted in 1977 was an adaptation of the flag of the *Ligue Populaire Africaine pour l'Indépendance* (LPAI), which led Djibouti to independence. The LPAI flag had a red triangle with a white star. For the national flag, adopted at independence, the star was placed in an upright, rather than a slanted position, and the proportions of the flag were lengthened. The colors stand for the Issas and the Afars, the two peoples of Djibouti at independence, and the red star for the unity of the diverse state.

The coat of arms is centered around a Somali shield and spear, bordered by two hunting knives.

ARMS OF DJIBOUTI

A Somali shield and weapons—two hunting knives and a spear

The red star is a traditional symbol of unity

The coat of arms contains a local shield

Ethiopia

Adopted October 31, 1996 | **Ratio** 1:2 | **Usage** National and Civil

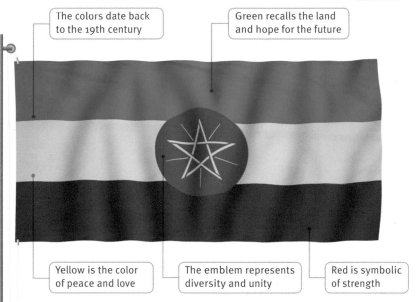

The colors date back to the 19th century

Green recalls the land and hope for the future

Yellow is the color of peace and love

The emblem represents diversity and unity

Red is symbolic of strength

Ethiopia was recognized as an empire in the 19th century. It was occupied by Italy from 1936–41. The Emperor was overthrown in 1974.

The three traditional colors—green, yellow, and red—date back to the Emperor Menelik (1889–1913) and were first used in a flag in 1895.

The current flag and emblem were adopted after the defeat of the Marxist Mengistu regime, in power from 1974–91. The emblem is intended to represent both the diversity and unity of the country.

ETHIOPIA AND THE RASTAFARI
In the 1930s the Ethiopian colors became popular with black activists in Jamaica who looked to Ethiopia for political and spiritual guidance. Since then, these colors (along with black from the flag of Marcus Garvey) have become linked with the Rastafarian movement, and have spread to other African countries.

EMBLEM OF ETHIOPIA

The star represents diversity and unity

Blue represents peace

The sun's rays symbolize prosperity

Somalia

Adopted October 12, 1954 | **Ratio** 2:3 | **Usage** National and Civil

The five-pointed star represents the branches of the Somali race—in Ethiopia, Kenya, Djibouti, and the former British and Italian colonies

The blue is the same as that used by the United Nations

Modern Somalia is a combination of a former Italian territory and British Somaliland. Since 1991 it has been in a state of civil war.

The flag was adopted by the Italian Trusteeship Territory in 1954 and was based on the blue and white flag of the United Nations, which was supervising the territory at the time. It was retained when Somalia became independent in 1960. The five-pointed star is said to stand for the five branches of the Somali race including those living in Ethiopia, Djibouti, and Kenya.

ARMS OF SOMALIA
The coat of arms was adopted in 1956. The leopards supporting the shield and the white star were also found on the arms used during the Italian administration.

ARMS OF SOMALIA

The shield is based on the national flag

Below the shield are two palm branches and two spears

The supporters are leopards; a leopard also featured on the shield of the colonial arms

Uganda

Adopted October 9, 1962 | **Ratio** 2:3 | **Usage** National and Civil

The colors of the flag represent the Ugandan people, sunlight, and brotherhood

Black, yellow, and red are the party colors of the UPC

The great crested crane is the national badge of Uganda

Since independence in 1962, Uganda has suffered years of upheaval. Under the current regime some stability has been restored.

The dominant party at the time of independence was the Uganda People's Congress (UPC), and the new national flag was an adaptation of its tricolor with the addition of the crane badge in the center. This dates back to before independence when the colonial badge of Uganda was the great crested crane. It also appears as one of the supporters on Uganda's coat of arms granted on September 3, 1962. The arms depicts a local shield, in an allegorical landscape with tea and cotton plants.

THE PRESIDENT'S STANDARD

The flag for the president was adopted in 1963 and consists of the arms on a red field with the national colors along the lower edge.

THE PRESIDENT'S STANDARD

A kob (a type of antelope) is one of the supporters

Coffee and cotton are Uganda's most important crops

A great crested crane also supports the shield

Blue and white represent the waters of the Nile and of Lake Victoria

Kenya

Adopted December 12, 1963 | **Ratio** 2:3 | **Usage** National and Civil

The white fimbriations were added to the KANU flag to create the national flag

White was added to represent the Kenya African Democratic Union

Red, black, and green are KANU party colors

The African shield is also used in the national arms

Kenya became a colony in 1920, previously called British East Africa. It became independent in 1963 and a republic in 1964.

The flag adopted at independence was based on that of the Kenya Africa National Union (KANU), the dominant political party. For the national flag, white fimbriations were added, and the shield and spears replaced the party symbol. A coat of arms, adopted in 1963, makes use of the same shield and spears, but with a white rooster in the center, grasping an ax.

Kenya was the first African country to use a shield of traditional design in its coat of arms, a practice which has since been followed in many other new states. It was also the first to give the motto in a local language, in this case Swahili.

ARMS OF KENYA

The shield stands on a representation of Kirinyaga (Mount Kenya)

The rooster with an ax is the KANU party symbol

Harambee meaning "Pull Together" in Swahili

Rwanda

Adopted December 31, 2001 | **Ratio** 2:3 | **Usage** National and Civil

Light blue stands for the hope of happiness and peace

Yellow is symbolic of the need for economic growth

Green represents future prosperity

The Golden Sun symbolizes the enlightenment that will bring unity and fight ignorance

Rwanda, originally part of German East Africa, was taken over by Belgium after the First World War. It became independent on July 1, 1962.

In 2001 Rwanda adopted a new national flag, national arms, and a national anthem, in response to the government's desire to concentrate on future possibilities rather than the troubled past. It was decided that the old national symbols reinforced the ideas of ethnic separatism and violence which eventually led to the genocide of 1994. For the new flag, red and black, which have often been associated with blood and mourning respectively, were removed, in favor of the more optimistic blue, yellow, and green. The new national symbols of Rwanda signify national unity, respect for work, patriotism, and confidence in the future.

ARMS OF RWANDA

The arms show a traditional hut, defended by shields

Emblems of agriculture and industry

The motto is Rwandan for "Unity, Work, Patriotism"

Everything is surrounded by a rope to show unity

Burundi

Adopted March 28, 1967 | **Ratio** 3:5 | **Usage** National and Civil

Red is symbolic of blood shed in the struggle for independence

The three stars represent the three ethnic groups, the Tutsi, Hutu, and Twa

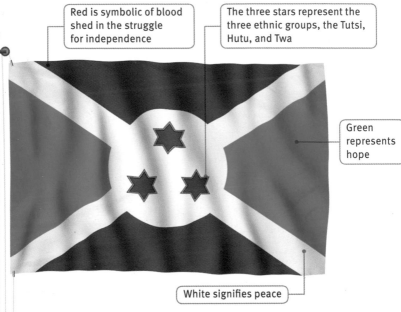

Green represents hope

White signifies peace

Like Rwanda, Burundi was a German, then a Belgian territory. It achieved independence as a kingdom in 1962 and became a republic in 1966.

The flag adopted at independence had a drum—symbolic of the monarchy—and a sorghum plant in the central disc. When the kingdom was abolished the drum was removed, and a year later the sorghum plant was replaced by the three stars, said to symbolize the main ethnic groups.

THE NATIONAL ARMS

The coat of arms has also been altered. The royal drum which was above the shield was removed; a more republican motto was adopted; and the four spears were reduced to three, again to represent the ethnic groups. The golden lion's face also featured on the royal badge.

ARMS OF BURUNDI

The lion's face has remained unchanged since the original 1962 arms

Three spears represent Burundi's ethnic groups

The motto is "*Unité-Travail-Progrès*," meaning "Unity, Work, Progress"

Central African Republic

Adopted December 1, 1958 | **Ratio** 3:5 | **Usage** National and Civil

The star represents hope of a union under France

Red, white, and blue are taken from the French *Tricolore*

Red, yellow, and green are Pan-African colors

The vertical stripe represents unity and the blood of humanity

Previously known as Ubangui-Shari, the Central African Republic was formed as an autonomous state in 1958 under French protection.

The flag is unique in that it combines the Pan-African colors with those of France, the former colonial power. This was done in the hope that neighboring states would join a federation under French protection, but this never materialized; the star represents the hope of achieving this goal. The state became an empire under the Emperor Bokassa from 1976–79, but no change was made to the national symbols.

The coat of arms is intended to symbolize both the Central African Republic and its important position in the center of Africa. The upper scroll bears the motto of the former ruling party; it means "A Man is a Man."

ARMS OF THE CENTRAL AFRICAN REPUBLIC

An elephant and a baobab tree

The national motto – *Unité, Dignité, Travail*, meaning "Unity, Dignity, Work"

The central feature is a gold star on a map of Africa, symbolizing the position of the Central African Republic

The hand was the party emblem of the ruling party in 1963, when the arms was adopted

Dem. Rep. of Congo

Adopted February 18, 2006 | **Ratio** 3:4 | **Usage** National and Civil

A blue flag with a yellow star was the flag of the Congo Free State from 1877–1908

The red diagonal represents the blood shed in civil wars

The gold fimbriations suggest hope in the future

The Democratic Republic of Congo was originally the Congo Free State (1880). In 1908 it became the Belgian Congo and then gained independence in 1960.

The flag of the Dem. Rep. of Congo is like the design used in 1963–71. The flag of the Congo Free State was blue with a central gold star. Under Belgian rule this flag remained, beside the Belgian flag. At independence in 1960, six stars were added down the hoist for the then six provinces. In 1964, the design changed to one like the present flag.

In 1971, the name of the country changed to Zaïre, and the flag was based on that of the ruling party. In 1997, the 1960 flag was restored, but replaced by the present design in 2006.

FLAG OF CONGO 1960–64 AND 1997–2006

FLAG OF ZAÏRE 1971–97

Niger

Adopted November 23, 1959 | **Ratio** 2:3 | **Usage** National and Civil

Orange represents the savannah grasslands

The orange disc is symbolic of the sun

White represents the river Niger

Green represents the country's rain forests

Niger was originally a province of French West Africa. In 1958, it joined the Sahel-Benin Union, achieving full independence in 1960.

The flag was designed in 1958 along with the Ivory Coast, with which Niger was in alliance, as well as Chad and Dahomey (modern Benin). This alliance came to nothing, but flags were adopted which indicated their common interest. In the case of Niger, the orange is said to stand for the savannah and the green for the rain forest, while the white strip stands for the Niger River, and the orange disc for the sun. The flag was retained on gaining independence and has remained unchanged ever since.

Four flags appear on the arms of Niger, surrounding a green or white shield. On the shield are weapons, the sun, a corncob, and a buffalo's head.

ARMS OF NIGER

Weapons represent military achievements

The title of the state—in French—is placed on the scroll

Corn represents the country's agriculture

The buffalo's head reflects pastoral farming

Chad

Adopted June 11, 1959 | **Ratio** 2:3 | **Usage** National and Civil

Blue symbolizes the sky and the waters of the south

Yellow symbolizes the sun and deserts

Red recalls the blood shed for independence

Chad became an autonomous republic in 1958 and for two years joined with Niger, Ivory Coast, and Dahomey in the informal Sahel-Benin Union.

The flag is a combination of the Pan-African colors popularized by Ghana, and those of the French *Tricolore*, on which it is closely modeled. It was adopted for the autonomous republic and retained on gaining independence in 1960. Despite many upheavals since independence the flag has not been changed.

THE NATIONAL ARMS
The coat of arms dates from 1970, although Chad also has a seal (like many former French colonies), adopted in 1959. The arms is in the colors of the national flag and is supported by a lion and a wild goat. The medal below the shield is the badge of the National Order of Chad.

ARMS OF CHAD

The red symbol is for salt, the country's main mineral

A mountain goat represents the north of Chad

The wavy bars symbolize Lake Chad

The lion is symbolic of the south of the country

The national motto— *"Unité, Travail, Progrès"* ("Unity, Work, Progress")

Mauritania

Adopted April 1, 1959 | **Ratio** 2:3 | **Usage** National and Civil

Green, representing the country's Islamic faith, and yellow are both Pan-African colors

The crescent and star of Islam

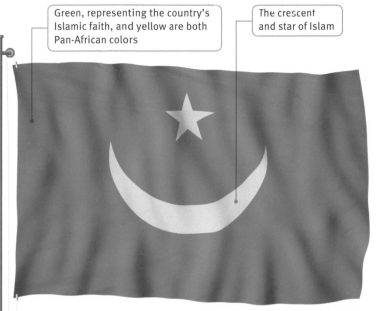

Mauritania became fully independent from France in 1960. From 1976–79 it occupied part of Western Sahara, now occupied by Morocco.

The flag was adopted in 1959 for the autonomous republic. It consists simply of a yellow crescent and star, a classic symbol of Islam, on a green field, expressive of the country's full title— "The Mauritanian Islamic Republic."

Mauritania also has a seal, like those used in many former French colonies. It is uncolored and represents a real seal, used for certifying documents.

It bears the title of the state around the edge. In the center are the Islamic crescent and star emblems. These are decorated with a palm branch and a millet plant, both important national plants. The seal was adopted for Mauritania in 1960.

SEAL OF MAURITANIA

The name of the country is given in both Arabic and French

The star and crescent of Islam

A palm branch

A millet plant

Mali

Adopted March 1, 1961 | **Ratio** 2:3 | **Usage** National and Civil

Green, yellow, and red are Pan-African colors

The style of the flag is modeled on the French *Tricolore*

Mali achieved independence from France in confederation with Senegal on June 20, 1960, but split away later the same year to form a republic.

The flag adopted in 1959 for the Confederation was an imitation of the flag of Ghana, but following the style of the French *Tricolore*. It was charged with a black emblem known as a *kanaga*, a stylized human figure. The colors were intended to reflect a unity with other African nations. After the two countries split up in 1960, the flag was kept for use in Mali until March 1, 1961, when the black figure was dropped.

Mali also has a seal, like those of other former French colonies. It is uncolored and displays a local fortress between two bows and arrows. Above the fortress is a dove of peace and below it is a rising sun in gold color.

SEAL OF MALI

The title of the state

The Great Mosque of Djenné, central Mali

A bow and arrow

The dove of peace

The national motto—"*Un Peuple, Un But, Une Foi*," meaning "One People, One Goal, One Faith"

Senegal

Adopted September, 1960 | **Ratio** 2:3 | **Usage** National and Civil

The Pan-African colors—green, yellow, and red

The star represents unity and hope

The design is modeled on a French *Tricolore*

Senegal achieved independence from France in federation with Mali in June 1960. The Federation lasted until August 1960.

The original flag for the Federation with Mali was adopted on April 4, 1959. It remained in use in Mali until March 1961.

A NEW NATIONAL FLAG

After the breakup of the Federation in 1960, Senegal adopted a new national flag, changing the black kanaga emblem on the original Federation flag to a green star representing unity and hope.

The coat of arms was designed by a French heraldist in 1965. It depicts a rampant lion and a baobab tree—emblems that had appeared on earlier badges of Senegal. The medal is the star of the National Order.

ARMS OF SENEGAL

The lion and baobab tree appeared on previous arms

A wreath of palm branches

The star of the National Order

The star is the same as that on the national flag

Motto is the same as Mali's—"*Un Peuple, Un But, Une Foi*" or "One People, One Goal, One Faith"

Gambia

Adopted February 18, 1965 | Ratio 2:3 | Usage National and Civil

Red represents the savannah grasslands

The blue stripe symbolizes the river Gambia

Green symbolizes the forests

The Gambia became self-governing in 1963, and fully independent of Britain on February 18, 1965. It became a republic on April 24, 1970.

The flag of the Gambia has no political basis. The blue stripe of the flag is said to represent the river Gambia flowing between the green forest and the red savannah. The flag was adopted at independence in 1965.

The coat of arms was granted before independence, in 1964. It makes no reference to the previous colonial badge of the Gambia and follows traditional heraldry. The two tools represent the main ethnic groups— the Mandinka and the Fulani— and the crest above the helmet is a local oil palm.

The federation formed with Senegal from 1981–89, but had no effect on the national symbols.

ARMS OF GAMBIA

The supporters are two lions, shown holding tools

A crest of oil palm leaves

An ax and a hoe represent the Mandinka and the Fulani, the two main ethnic groups in the Gambia

The national motto— "Progress, Peace, Prosperity"

Cape Verde

Adopted September 22, 1992 | **Ratio** 2:3 | **Usage** National and Civil

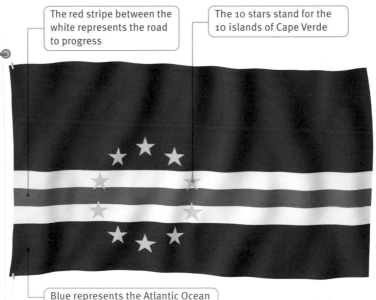

The red stripe between the white represents the road to progress

The 10 stars stand for the 10 islands of Cape Verde

Blue represents the Atlantic Ocean

Cape Verde was originally an overseas province of Portugal. It obtained independence in 1975. In 1992 a multiparty Constitution was adopted.

The original flag, adopted in 1975, was very similar to that of Guinea-Bissau, both were based on the flag of the same dominant political party.

The current flag, adopted by the new government in 1992, depicts the ocean in blue, with the islands as a ring of stars on a line of red fimbriated in white, representing the road to progress. The stars may be derived from the arms of Praia, the capital.

The national arms depicts a torch on a triangle, symbolizing unity and freedom. It also includes the ring of stars and a plumb-bob signifying rectitude and virtue, which are the "keystones" of the Constitution.

ARMS OF CAPE VERDE

The title of the state

The stars represent the main islands of Cape Verde

REPÚBLICA DE CABO VERDE

The plumb-bob is symbolic of rectitude and virtue

The torch and triangle represent unity and freedom

Guinea-Bissau

Adopted September 24, 1973 | **Ratio** 1:2 | **Usage** National and Civil

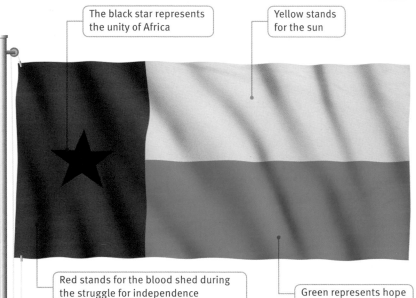

The black star represents the unity of Africa

Yellow stands for the sun

Red stands for the blood shed during the struggle for independence

Green represents hope

Guinea-Bissau is so called to distinguish it from the former French Guinea. Once a territory of Portugal, it achieved self-government in 1973.

Like the former flag of Cape Verde, the flag is based on that of the *Partido Africano para a Independencia da Guiné e Cabo Verde* (PAIGC), still the dominant party in Guinea-Bissau.

THE GHANAIAN INFLUENCE

The party flag was derived from that of Ghana, which first used the Pan-African combination of red, yellow, green, and black in 1957. In the Ghanaian view, the black star stands for the unity of Africa. The colors are now said to stand for the blood that was shed for independence, hope, and the sun as the source of life.

The coat of arms is the PAIGC badge, a black star and a scallop shell.

ARMS OF GUINEA-BISSAU

A star symbolizing African unity

As the PAIGC badge, the palm leaves represent Guinea-Bissau

The PAIGC motto—*"Unidade, Luta, Progresso,"* meaning "Unity, Struggle, Progress"

The scallop shell originally recalled the Cape Verde islands

Guinea

Adopted November 10, 1958 | **Ratio** 2:3 | **Usage** National and Civil

The flag is modeled on the French *Tricolore*, but in Pan-African colors

Yellow represents the sun and the riches of the earth

Green represents the country's vegetation

Red symbolizes the people's sacrifice

In 1958, Guinea became the first territory in former French West Africa to gain independence without first becoming an autonomous republic.

The colors of the flag were adapted from those of the *Rassemblement Démocratique Africaine*, the dominant movement at the time of independence. Their colors, first adopted in 1957, were, in turn, derived from those of Ghana. Sekou Touré, the first President of Guinea, was a close associate of Kwame Nkrumah, the former dictator of Ghana.

ARMS OF GUINEA
The coat of arms has been altered since the fall of Sekou Touré. The elephant's head was dropped, as were the crossed weapons in 2011, and now it simply portrays a dove carrying an olive branch in its beak.

ARMS OF GUINEA

The dove is a symbol of peace

The national motto— "*Travail, Justice, Solidarité,*" meaning "Work, Justice, Solidarity"

The olive branch symbolizes peace

Sierra Leone

Adopted April 27, 1961 | **Ratio** 2:3 | **Usage** National and Civil

Green represents the agricultural and natural resources of the country

Blue recalls the natural harbour at Freetown, the capital

White stands for justice

Sierra Leone was founded as a home for freed slaves in 1787, but became a British colony in 1808. It achieved independence in 1961.

The arms and flag of Sierra Leone, granted in 1960, were devised by the College of Arms in Britain.

ARMS OF SIERRA LEONE
The shield depicts a lion beneath a zigzag border, representing the "Lion Mountains" after which the territory was named, and three torches. At the base are wavy bars depicting the sea. The supporters are lions, which are similar to those on the colonial badge.

The three main colors from the shield—green, white, and blue—were used to form the flag. They represent agricultural and natural resources in green, unity and justice in white, and blue for the harbor at Freetown.

ARMS OF SIERRA LEONE

The lions holding oil palms are taken from the old colonial badge

National motto—
"*Unity, Freedom, Justice*"

The torches symbolize education and progress

The border represents the "Lion Mountains"

The wavy bars depict the sea

Liberia

Adopted July 26, 1847 | **Ratio** 10:19 | **Usage** National and Civil

Eleven stripes represent the 11 men who signed the Liberian Declaration of Independence

The flag is modeled on the Stars and Stripes of the USA

The star represents African freedom

Liberia was founded in 1816 by the American Colonization Society as a home for freed slaves from the USA. It became independent in 1847.

The flag of Liberia is clearly based on that of the USA, with one white star in a blue canton standing for the freedom it was intended should shine forth in the so-called "Dark Continent." The canton itself represents Africa. The 11 stripes are said to stand, in this case, for the signatories of Liberia's Declaration of Independence. All the counties of Liberia have local flags, but the extent of their use is unclear.

ARMS OF LIBERIA
The shield depicts a ship bringing freed slaves from the USA. The rising sun in the background represents the birth of a nation, and a palm tree indicates prosperity. A white dove symbolizes peace.

ARMS OF LIBERIA

White dove symbolizes peace

The palm tree represents prosperity

The rising sun represents the birth of a nation

A plough indicates the value of hard work

Ivory Coast

Adopted December 3, 1959 | **Ratio** 2:3 | **Usage** National and Civil

Orange represents the savannah grasslands

White represents the country's rivers

Green recalls the coastal forests

Ivory Coast was originally part of French West Africa. It became independent in its own right on August 7, 1960.

After independence, Ivory Coast formed a loose alliance of West African states. The flags of these states were influenced both by the Pan-African colors first used by Ghana, and also by the model of the French *Tricolore*, the flag of the former colonial power.

ALLIANCE OF WEST AFRICAN STATES
The colors chosen for Ivory Coast's flag were also used by Niger, with which Ivory Coast had an alliance (the resemblance to the colors of Ireland is coincidental). They were intended to symbolize the following: orange represents the savannah grasslands, white the rivers, and green the coastal forests. Another interpretation is that

they symbolize progress, hope, and national unity. The flag was adopted in 1959, just prior to independence.

THE NATIONAL ARMS
The coat of arms, which has a green shield charged with an elephant's head, is based on the emblem of the *Rassemblement Démocratique Africaine*, the dominant political party at the time of independence. Originally the elephant's head was on a blue shield, but this was altered in 1964 to green to match the national flag. The shield is supported by two palm trees, behind which is a rising sun. On a scroll at the base of the arms is the title of the state, "*Republique de Côte d'Ivoire*."

Burkina

Adopted August 4, 1984 | **Ratio** 2:3 | **Usage** National and Civil

Red recalls the 1984 revolution

The star is the guiding light of the revolution

Green represents Burkina's abundant natural resources

Burkina, originally known as Upper Volta, was once a French colony. It became self-governing in 1958 and fully independent in 1960.

The original flag of Upper Volta, adopted at independence, contained three horizontal stripes of black, white, and red. These simple colors represented the three major tributaries of the Volta River, which flow south through the country.

A NEW NATIONAL FLAG

In August 1984 there was a coup, and a new flag and emblem were adopted. The new flag is in the Pan-African colors, reflecting both a break with the country's colonial past and its unity with other African ex-colonies. The red is also said to symbolize the revolution and the green the abundance of natural riches. The yellow star placed over the red and green stripes is the guiding light of the revolution.

THE NATIONAL ARMS

The coat of arms, which was adopted in September 1997, shows a shield in the colors of the national flag. The arms are held by two horses, which represent the nobility of the people. Two crossed lances show the will of the people to defend their country, and an open book and two ears of millet symbolize their will to educate and feed themselves. At the top of the arms is a scroll inscribed with the name Burkina Faso—the country of the upright people. At the base, another scroll carries the national motto: Unity, Development, Justice.

Ghana

Adopted March 6, 1957 | **Ratio** 2:3 | **Usage** National

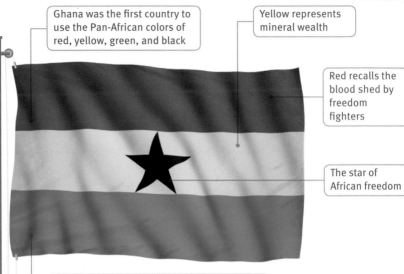

Ghana was the first country to use the Pan-African colors of red, yellow, green, and black

Yellow represents mineral wealth

Red recalls the blood shed by freedom fighters

The star of African freedom

Green is symbolic of the country's rich forests

Previously the Gold Coast, Ghana became independent from Britain in 1957. It took its new name from that of an historic African empire.

Kwame Nkrumah, Ghana's first leader after independence, was the first to introduce the politically symbolic Pan-African colors—red, yellow, green, and black—into African flags. They were ultimately derived from the colors of Ethiopia, dating back to the 19th century, and have now become associated with the Rastafarian movement in the West Indies. The flag also became the inspiration for numerous other African flags during the period of decolonization.

Ghana followed the flag patterns established in the United Kingdom, and so has a both a red ensign for use on civil vessels and a white ensign for naval vessels. This use of several flags sets it apart from other West African states, which normally have only one all-purpose flag.

GHANAIAN RED ENSIGN

The national flag is placed in the canton

The field is in the style of the British Red Ensign

Togo

Adopted April 27, 1960 | **Ratio** 2:3 | **Usage** National and Civil

Red symbolizes the blood shed during the struggle for independence

Yellow reflects Togo's mineral wealth

The star of hope

Green represents agricultural wealth

Togo, once a German colony, was divided between France and Britain in 1914. The French part became independent, as Togo, in 1960.

During 1956–60, the period of autonomy, the flag was green with two yellow stars arranged diagonally. Between 1957–58, the French *Tricolore* was in the canton.

On independence in 1960, the present flag was adopted. The five stripes stand for the regions of Togo, and are in green and yellow to signify its agricultural and mineral resources. The red canton is for the blood of those who struggled for independence, while the white star is for hope, as on Liberia's flag. The national emblem contains two lions holding bows and arrows, and a sun with the country's initials, with the national motto above it.

EMBLEM OF TOGO

"RT" stands for the title of the state, *République Togolaise*

The national motto— "*Union, Paix, Solidarité*"—meaning "Unity, Peace, Solidarity"

Two lions are shown carrying bows and arrows to protect the homeland

Benin

Adopted November 16, 1959 | **Ratio** 2:3 | **Usage** National and Civil

Red, yellow, and green symbolize African unity and nationalism

Originally known as Dahomey, Benin became autonomous in 1958 and independent from France in 1960. Its name was changed in 1975.

The flag used today is the same as that adopted in 1959, although after the revolution of December 1975, a green flag with a red star in the canton was used. The original flag was restored in 1990, as was the original national emblem. The new name of the country was retained.

Benin has both a seal and a coat of arms. The seal depicts a *pirogue* or African canoe, with a bow and arrow, and two clubs. The arms consists of a quartered shield depicting a local Somba fortress, the medal of the Order of the Star of Benin, a palm tree, and a sailing ship. The motto is "*Fraternité, Justice, Travail*," meaning "Fraternity, Justice, Work."

ARMS OF BENIN

A Somba fortress

The national motto, meaning "Fraternity, Justice, Work"

The Horns of Plenty spilling out ears of corn are symbolic of riches from the land

The Order of Star of Benin

Nigeria

Adopted October 1, 1960 | **Ratio** 1:2 | **Usage** National

Green recalls the land

White symbolizes peace and unity

Nigeria was formed in 1914 from several British colonies and protectorates. In 1954 it became a federation and in 1960 achieved independence.

The national flag is an adaptation of the winning entry in a competition held in 1959. The original had a red sun with streaming rays placed at the top of the white stripe. This was removed by the judges and the flag has not been altered since. Like Ghana, Nigeria has special flags for civil and naval vessels, and at one time the states also had flags. The coat of arms was granted in 1960, but the motto has been altered since then to include the words "Peace and Progress." The shield represents the confluence of two rivers and the crest is a red eagle. It all stands on a green base strewn with the *Costus Spectabilis* flower.

ARMS OF NIGERIA

The confluence of the Niger and Benuë rivers

The *Costus Spectabilis* is the national flower

The national motto— "Unity and Faith, Peace, and Progress"

The red eagle, symbolizing strength, is the national badge

The two white horses symbolize dignity

Cameroon

Adopted May 20, 1975 | **Ratio** 2:3 | **Usage** National and Civil

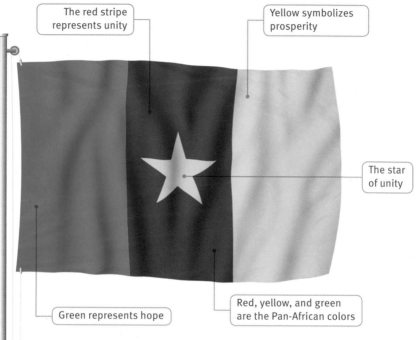

The red stripe represents unity

Yellow symbolizes prosperity

The star of unity

Green represents hope

Red, yellow, and green are the Pan-African colors

Cameroon was originally a German colony, which was partitioned by the French and the British after the First World War.

The French area became autonomous on January 1, 1959, and independent a year later. A national flag was adopted during the period of French control and was the first West African flag after that of Ghana to use the red, yellow, and green colors. The actual design is based on the French *Tricolore*. The original design of 1959 did not have a star.

A NEW UNITED FLAG
In 1961, the southern part of British Cameroon joined the former French colony forming the current state of Cameroon. To mark this, two yellow stars were placed in the upper hoist. In 1975, the two stars were replaced by a

single star in the center of the flag to symbolize the new unity of the state.

THE NATIONAL ARMS
The coat of arms, like the flag, has been altered to reflect the changes in the constitution. The date of independence of French Cameroon has been removed, leaving just the name of the state on the scroll and there is now only one yellow star in the red on the shield. The main features of the current arms are a map of the country, a set of scales, and two crossed fasces or local axes. The shield is divided in the colors of the national flag—green, red, and yellow.

Equatorial Guinea

Adopted October 12, 1968 | **Ratio** 2:3 | **Usage** National and Civil

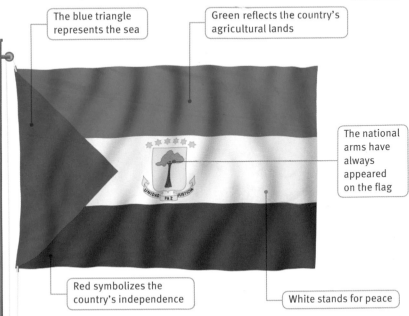

The blue triangle represents the sea

Green reflects the country's agricultural lands

The national arms have always appeared on the flag

Red symbolizes the country's independence

White stands for peace

Equatorial Guinea includes the former Spanish colonies of Río Muni, the island of Fernando Po (Bioko), and other islands in the Gulf of Guinea.

The flag was first shown on the day of independence, October 12, 1968, and has always contained the national emblem in the center, although starting in 1972, a different national emblem appeared on the flag during the regime of Francisco Nguema. The original coat of arms was restored after he was deposed in August 1979.

ARMS OF EQUATORIAL GUINEA

The arms consists of a silver shield charged with a silk cotton tree, which was derived from the arms of Río Muni. Above the shield is an arc of six, six-pointed stars, which represent Río Muni and the offshore islands. Beneath the shield is a scroll bearing the national motto.

ARMS OF EQUATORIAL GUINEA

The six stars stand for the six parts of the state

A silk cotton tree

The national motto— *"Unidad, Paz, Justicia"* ("Unity, Peace, Justice")

A silver shield

São Tomé & Príncipe

Adopted November 5, 1975 | **Ratio** 1:2 | **Usage** National and Civil

Green, red, yellow, and black are Pan-African colors

The two stars stand for the two islands

The red triangle recalls the struggle for independence, as on the flags of Ghana and Togo

São Tomé & Príncipe are a pair of islands in the Gulf of Guinea that formerly belonged to Portugal. They became independent in 1975.

The flag is based on the party flag of the Movement for the Liberation of São Tomé & Príncipe (MLSTP). It was retained even after the party lost its monopoly of power in 1990.

The combination of red, yellow, and green with black stars is clearly based on the flag of Ghana, with the stars representing the two islands.

The shield within the national arms is in the form of a cocoa pod, on which is depicted a cocoa palm, the country's main export. Above this is a star representing freedom. The supporters are two pigeons standing on a scroll with the national motto—"*Unidade, Disciplina, Trabajo*" ("Unity, Discipline, Work").

ARMS OF SÃO TOMÉ & PRÍNCIPE

The crest, a blue star, stands for African freedom

The upper scroll bears the title of the state

The shield is supported by a falcon on the left and a parrot on the right

The shield is in the form of a cocoa pod

Gabon

Adopted August 9, 1960 | **Ratio** 3:4 | **Usage** National and Civil

Yellow and green represent natural resources

Blue represents the sea

Gabon was once a province of French Equatorial Africa. It became independent in 1960 under the leadership of the Gabon Democratic Party.

The original flag was adopted in 1959 and was similar to the present one, but with stripes of unequal width and the French *Tricolore* in the canton. The *Tricolore* was dropped at independence. The flag's unusual proportions are laid down by law and the colors are said to stand for the sea, and for the country's natural resources, especially its timber.

The coat of arms is in European style and is the colors of the flag. The shield is supported by two black panthers and an okoumé tree, symbolic of the timber trade. The coat of arms is unusual in having a Latin motto— "*Uniti Progrediamur*"—beneath the branches of the tree.

ARMS OF GABON

A Latin motto— "*Unite Progrediamur*"— meaning "We go forward in unity"

A second motto means "Union, Work, Justice"

The *okoumé* tree is symbolic of the timber trade

Two black panthers support the shield

The ship represents Gabon moving toward a brighter future

Congo

Adopted September 15, 1959 | **Ratio** 2:3 | **Usage** National and Civil

The Pan-African colors of green, yellow, and red

The distinctive diagonal pattern sets it apart from other Pan-African flags

Congo was a French colony known as Congo-Brazzaville until independence in 1960. After a coup in 1964, it became the People's Republic (1970–91).

The current flag was originally adopted for the autonomous republic, established on August 18, 1959. It is in the Pan-African colors used by many other West African flags. It was retained without change when full independence was achieved in 1960.

THE PEOPLE'S REPUBLIC 1970–91

Following the Marxist revolution in 1964, no new national flag was officially adopted until the People's Republic was formed in 1970. This flag was red and contained the national emblem in the canton. The emblem depicted a wreath containing a crossed hoe and hammer, and a gold star. This represented the communist regime which had taken power.

AN OLD FLAG FOR A NEW ERA

At the National Conference for the restoration of democracy in 1991, which restored a multiparty democracy, it was decided to readopt the original flag, arms and national anthem. This decision was made official on June 4, 1991.

ARMS OF CONGO

The coat of arms was originally adopted in 1963 and was designed by the European heraldist Louis Mühlemann, who also designed the arms of Gabon. It follows a traditional European heraldic style.

Angola

Adopted November 11, 1975 | **Ratio** 2:3 | **Usage** National and Civil

The design is based on flag of the MPLA

The cogwheel and machete represent agriculture and industry, and are similar to the Soviet-style hammer and sickle

Originally a Portuguese colony, Angola was eventually liberated by the People's Liberation Movement of Angola in 1975.

The flag of the People's Liberation Movement of Angola (MPLA) is like the present national flag but with a yellow star. The half cogwheel and machete on the national flag were added to create an emblem reminiscent of the hammer and sickle on the Soviet flag.

The national arms also features the cogwheel, star, and machete, but includes a hoe. These symbols are on a background which, like the emblem on the flag, is similar to the devices used in Soviet designs. The cogwheel is balanced by a wreath of cotton, coffee, and corn, and an open book. On the scroll is "Republic of Angola," the state name.

ARMS OF ANGOLA

The tools are emblems of agriculture and of industry

The book is symbolic of the importance of education

The Soviet-style emblem is still in use

The state name, in Portuguese—*República de Angola*—is placed on the scroll

Zambia

Adopted October 24, 1964 | **Ratio** 2:3 | **Usage** National and Civil

The green field represents Zambia's agriculture

The eagle is taken from the national arms

Orange represents the country's copper

Black stands for the people

Red recalls the struggle for independence

Zambia was formerly the British colony of Northern Rhodesia. It was granted full independence in 1964.

Although the United National Independence Party is no longer dominant in Zambia, the party's colors remain in the bottom corner of the flag, designed by graphic artists just prior to independence. The eagle is taken from the national arms, which are based on those of the former Northern Rhodesia.

In the arms, the eagle, which once appeared in the upper part of the shield, forms the crest, above a crossed pickax and hoe. White and black bars on the shield represent the famous Victoria Falls. The supporters are an African man and woman, and the motto on the base reads "One Zambia, One Nation."

ARMS OF ZAMBIA

The pickax and hoe are emblems of agriculture and industry

The shield stands on an allegorical landscape

The eagle of liberty

The shield represents the white waters of the Zambezi River flowing over black rock at the Victoria Falls

ONE ZAMBIA   ONE NATION

Tanzania

Adopted June 30, 1964 | **Ratio** 2:3 | **Usage** National and Civil

Green and black, taken from the old Tanganyikan flag, represent the land and the people

Yellow symbolizes mineral wealth

Blue, taken from the flag of Zanzibar, represents the sea

The British Trusteeship Territory of Tanganyika became independent in 1961. In 1964, it merged with the Republic of Zanzibar, to form Tanzania.

The original flag of independent Tanganyika featured horizontal stripes of green-black-green derived from the flag of Tanganyika African National Union, the dominant party at the time. For the national flag, yellow fimbriations were placed between the green and the black. Derived from the Afro-Shirazi Party, the flag of Zanzibar is green, black, and blue stripes, with a vertical white stripe along the hoist.

A NEW UNITED FLAG

When the two countries united to form Tanzania, a new national flag was created, which combined the colors of Tanganyika and Zanzibar. The country's coat of arms was also altered to include the new national flag in the shield, again to reflect the new union of the two countries.

FLAG OF ZANZIBAR

The national flag was added as a canton to the revolutionary flag of 1964

These are the colors of the Afro-Shirazi Party, which overthrew the ruling Sultan in 1964

Malawi

Adopted July 6, 1964 | **Ratio** 2:3 | **Usage** National and Civil

These are the colors of the Malawi Congress Party

The rising sun symbolizes a new dawn

Black is symbolic of Malawi's African heritage

Red represents the blood shed for freedom

Green represents the land

As Nyasaland, Malawi formed part of British Rhodesia and Nyasaland from 1953–63. It became fully independent in 1964.

The colors of the flag are the same as those of Malawi Congress Party (MCP), which led the country to independence in 1964. The MCP flag was derived from the flag popularized by Marcus Garvey at the time of the First World War, as the flag of Africa, or "Ethiopia," symbolizing an African renaissance. For Malawi's national flag the rising sun, or *kwacha*, was added in red. In 2010, the design was altered to reflect the Pan-African layout, and a white sun was added to the center. A public outcry ensued, and the flag was finally changed back in 2012 by the new president.

THE PRESIDENT'S FLAG
The flag of the president has a bright red field. It uses the lion passant found in the center of the coat of arms.

THE PRESIDENT'S FLAG

The name of the state

The lion passant is taken from the coat of arms

Zimbabwe

Adopted April 18, 1980 | **Ratio** 1:2 | **Usage** National and Civil

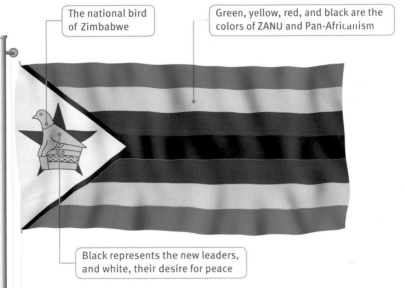

The national bird of Zimbabwe

Green, yellow, red, and black are the colors of ZANU and Pan-Africanism

Black represents the new leaders, and white, their desire for peace

Zimbabwe, the name of an ancient African city, is now applied to the whole country, which was formerly known as Rhodesia.

The Zimbabwe African National Union (ZANU) led the struggle for self-determination in the 1970s, and its flag was used as the basis for the new national flag. The ZANU flag is composed of concentric panels of green, yellow, red, with a central black panel—the colors of Pan-Africanism. The national flag has these colors simply arranged in stripes. Toward the hoist is a white triangle with a black edge, symbolizing new leaders and their desire for peace. Within this is the Zimbabwe bird on a red star.

THE ZIMBABWE BIRD
The bird is representative of birds found in the ruins of the ancient city of Zimbabwe and has been a local symbol since 1924. The star stands for an international outlook.

EMBLEM OF ZIMBABWE

The star represents the country's international outlook

The Zimbabwe bird

A representation of the ancient city of Zimbabwe

Mozambique

Adopted May 1, 1983 | **Ratio** 2:3 | **Usage** National and Civil

Red recalls the struggle for independence

Green symbolizes the riches of the land

Black recalls the African continent

Yellow symbolizes the country's minerals

The white fimbriations represent peace

Mozambique was a Portuguese colony before becoming independent under the single-party rule of FRELIMO in 1975.

The original flag of the *Frente da Libertação da Moçambique* (FRELIMO), the leading political party in Mozambique, also had green, black, and yellow horizontal stripes separated by white fimbriations. In the hoist was a red triangle. The black, green, and yellow were derived from the flag of the African National Congress, used in South Africa.

On independence the colors were rearranged to form the national flag, in rays emanating from the upper hoist. Over this was a white cogwheel containing the hoe, rifle, book, and star, which appear on the present flag. The flag was altered in 1983—the colors were arranged in horizontal stripes, and the star of Marxism was made larger.

EMBLEM OF MOZAMBIQUE

The hoe represents the country's agriculture

The rifle stands for defense and vigilance

The star symbolizes Marxism and internationalism

The open book symbolizes the importance of education

Namibia

Adopted March 21, 1990 | **Ratio** 2:3 | **Usage** National and Civil

The sun is the emblem of life and energy

Red, white, and blue were the colors of the Democratic Turnhalle Alliance

Blue, red, and green were the colors of SWAPO

Namibia, once German South West Africa, passed into South African control after World War I, until gaining independence in 1990.

The national flag combines the colors of the South West African People's Organization (SWAPO), which liberated Namibia in 1990, and those of the Democratic Turnhalle Alliance, another Namibian political party. The sun, which is similar to that on the flag of Taiwan, is said to stand for life and energy.

ARMS OF NAMIBIA

The coat of arms, adopted with the flag, appears on the President's Flag. The shield is of the same pattern as the national flag, and is supported by a pair of oryx. On a sand dune beneath is a *welwitschia* plant, found in the Namib Desert. The crest is a fish eagle on a chieftain's headring.

ARMS OF NAMIBIA

The shield is based on the national flag

The fish eagle stands on a chieftain's headring

Two oryx support the shield

The national motto—"Unity, Liberty, Justice"

The *welwitschia* plant is found in the Namib Desert

Botswana

Adopted September 30, 1966 | **Ratio** 2:3 | **Usage** National and Civil

Black and white symbolize the harmony of the people

Blue represents both water and life

Botswana, originally known as British Bechuanaland, is now known by its Setswana name. Independence was achieved in 1966.

Prior to its independence, Botswana did not have its own distinctive flag. The flag was designed to contrast with the South African flag, in reaction to the neighboring country being ruled under an apartheid regime. As a result, the national flag of Botswana does not use the Pan-African colors. Neither is it derived from that of the dominant political party. The new flag was flown for the first time at midnight on the day independence was declared.

PULA—LIFE-GIVING RAIN
The flag is based on the idea of life-giving rain, an essential element in the drought-prone country. This is also reflected in the Setswana word *pula*, which forms the national motto. This means not only "water" and "rain" but also the life that is derived from it. The two horizontal blue stripes

represent rain and water. The importance of water is also a feature on the flag of Lesotho. The black stripe fimbriated with white in the center of the flag represents the idea of the African and European populations of Botswana living together in harmony.

ARMS OF BOTSWANA
The coat of arms, which appears on the President's Flag was adopted in 1966. The African shield depicts three cogwheels and a bull's head separated by three wavy bars of water. The supporters are two zebras, holding an elephant tusk and the other a sorghum plant, the country's staple crop. Some also interpret the zebras, with their black and white stripes, as being symbolic of racial integration.

Lesotho

Adopted October 4, 2006 | **Ratio** 2:3 | **Usage** National and Civil

A black *mokorotlo* (Basotho hat) represents the people

Blue is symbolic of the importance of water and rain

White represents peace

Green represents plenty

Lesotho was formerly known as British Basutoland but is now known by its Sesotho name. It became independent in 1966.

The national flag was changed to commemorate the fortieth anniversary of independence. The change from a shield to a black *mokorotlo*, a Basotho hat, reflects a peaceful future for the country.

ARMS OF LESOTHO
The shield, of African design, contains a crocodile, which is a symbol of King Moshoeshoe I, who founded the state in 1824.

It stands on a representation of Mount Thaba Bosiu, the Mountain of Night, and is supported by two Basuto ponies. Behind the shield is a spear and a knobkerrie, a local club.

The national motto at the base reads *Khotso, Pula, Nala* which translates as "Peace, Rain, Prosperity."

ARMS OF LESOTHO

The shield stands on a representation of Thaba Bosigo

Two Basuto ponies support the shield

A crocodile, symbol of King Moshoeshoe I

Swaziland

Adopted October 1, 1968 | **Ratio** 2:3 | **Usage** National and Civil

Injobo tassels, made from widowbird and lourie feathers

Assegais are Swazi spears

The pattern of the shield is taken from the Emasotsha Regiment

Swaziland was a British Protectorate until 1968. It is now ruled by the Swazi royal family, who founded the kingdom in the 19th century.

The flag is based on one given by the late King Sobhuza II to the Swazi Pioneer Corps in 1941. On it is an Emasotsha shield, laid horizontally. The shield is reinforced by a staff from which hang *injobo* tassels; bunches of feathers of the widowbird and the lourie. They also decorate the shield. Above the staff are two *assegais*—local spears. The shield and *assegais* appear on the national arms, which is supported by a lion and an elephant, symbolic of the King and of the Queen Mother. The crest is an otterskin headdress decorated with widowbird feathers, and the motto is *Siyinqaba* meaning "We are the fortress."

ARMS OF SWAZILAND

A lion, symbolic of the King

A headdress with widowbird feathers

The national motto—"We are the fortress"

An elephant, symbolic of the Queen Mother

South Africa

Adopted April 27, 1994 | **Ratio** 2:3 | **Usage** National and Civil

The overall design conveys convergence and unification

Green, black, and yellow are taken from the ANC flag

Red, white, and blue are taken from the colors of the Boer republics

The Union of South Africa was formed in 1910 and the republic in 1961. In 1994 a democratic, multiracial constitution was adopted.

South Africa had no distinctive flag until 1928 when a national flag was adopted based on the orange, white, and blue tricolor used by the first Dutch settlers, with three smaller flags in the center for Britain, Transvaal, and the Orange Free State.

A NEW FLAG FOR A NEW ERA

When a multiracial democracy came into being, attempts were made to find a new flag and the present design, created by the Chief Herald of South Africa, was adopted.

The new South African flag combines the colors of the Boer republics with those of the African National Congress (ANC), whose flag was adopted in 1917. The Y-shape represents the convergence of old traditions with new and the progress of the united state into the future.

ARMS OF SOUTH AFRICA

Tusks are for strength and eternity

Motto is in the earliest known (though now extinct) language in South Africa; it translates as "Diverse People Unite"

The secretary bird spreads its wings to show the ascent of the nation

The weapons of war symbolize defense, but are laid down, symbolizing peace

Seychelles

Adopted June 18, 1996 | **Ratio** 1:2 | **Usage** National and Civil

Blue and yellow are the colors of the Democratic Party

Red, white, and green are the colors of the SPUP

The Seychelles became independent from France in 1976. In 1977, a coup d'état brought the Seychelles People's United Party to power.

The Seychelles has had three flags since independence. After the coup of 1977, a new national flag, based on the party flag of the ruling SPUP, was adopted. This used their colors of red, white, and green.

Following the adoption of the Constitution of 1993, the existence of other parties was permitted and so the latest flag allows for the colors of the Democratic Party to be included in a striking new design.

The coat of arms was adopted in 1976 and it has been only slightly altered since then. It is based on the old colonial badge and depicts the most famous inhabitant of the islands, the giant tortoise.

ARMS OF THE SEYCHELLES

Two sailfish support the arms

A Latin motto—*Finis Coronat Opus*, meaning "The end crowns the work," was chosen in the 19th century

The crest is a *paille-en-queue*—a native bird of the Seychelles

The giant tortoise and palm have been in use in the arms since the 19th century

Comoros

Adopted January 7, 2002 | **Ratio** 3:5 | **Usage** Government and Civil

The crescent of Islam

Four stars represent the four islands of the Comoros

Each stripe represents one of the four islands

Green is the traditional color of Islam

The Comoros became independent in 1975, although the island of Mayotte did not join the new state and remains a French dependency.

The present flag is based on one adopted at independence, which included stars for the four main islands (including Mayotte) and a crescent to symbolize Islam.

The original flag was mainly red, to underline the socialist aspirations of the country. This was dropped in 1978 in favor of a green flag, with the crescent and stars in white. The Constitution of 1996 modified the flag to include the monograms of Allah and of Muhammad in the top right and bottom left corners.

Comoros adopted a new name, constitution, and flag in January 2002. The four stars, the crescent moon, and the green of Islam have been moved into a triangle. Each stripe of yellow, white, red, and blue represents one of the four islands.

THE NATIONAL FLAG 1996–2002

A monogram of Allah

A monogram of the Prophet Muhammad

Madagascar

Adopted October 14, 1958 | **Ratio** 2:3 | **Usage** National and Civil

White and red were the colors of the Kingdom of Madagascar

Green represents the Hova, the former peasant class

Madagascar was annexed by France in 1895 and the monarchy abolished two years later. It achieved independence in 1960.

The flag was introduced when self-government was achieved in 1958 and was retained on independence. The red and white are said to symbolize the earlier Merina Kingdom, whose flags were all red and white, with the addition of green for the Hova, the former peasant class. The seal has changed several times since independence. That of the present republic, introduced in March 1993, shows a map of the island with a spray of leaves. Beneath these is a paddy field surmounted by the head of a zebu. The motto reads "Fatherland, Liberty, Justice." Above the design is the country's name.

SEAL OF MADAGASCAR

The leaves of the traveler's tree

The national motto—"Fatherland, Liberty, Justice"

The state title is in Malagasy, the local language

An outline of Madagascar

A stylized paddy field and a zebu—a local ox

Mauritius

Adopted January 9, 1968 | **Ratio** 2:3 | **Usage** National

Red reflects independence

Blue is the color of the Indian Ocean

Yellow symbolizes a bright future

Green recalls the lush vegetation of the island

Mauritius was taken over by Britain from France in 1810. The colony achieved independence in 1968 and became a republic in 1992.

The flag was designed by the College of Arms in Britain prior to independence, and is a simple statement of the colors found in the coat of arms.

MAURITIUS'S COAT OF ARMS

The coat of arms was granted on August 25, 1906, and depicts various attributes of the island. In the lower right quarter is a key and on the left-hand side is a white star, which are referred to in the Latin motto *Stella Clavisque Maris Indici* ("The star and the key of the Indian Ocean"). The supporters are a dodo and a deer each holding a sugar cane, the island's staple crop.

ARMS OF MAURITIUS

A dodo, extinct since the 18th century

A ship symbolizing colonization

Palm trees represent the country's tropical vegetation

The national motto—"The star and the key of the Indian Ocean"

The star and key are referred to in the motto

Europe

Iceland

Adopted June 19, 1915 | **Ratio** 18:25 | **Usage** National and Civil

White recalls the ice and snow that covers Iceland

Deep blue represents the Atlantic Ocean

Red represents the fire produced by the island's volcanoes

Ruled by the Danes in the 14th century, Iceland became a realm within the kingdom of Denmark in 1918, and a republic in 1944.

Iceland's first national flag was a white cross on a deep blue background. It was first paraded in 1897. The modern flag dates from 1915, when a red cross was inserted into the white cross of the original flag.

It was adopted in 1918 and became the national flag when Iceland gained independence from Denmark in 1944.

The naval ensign is swallow-tailed, as are the naval ensigns of all the Scandinavian countries.

NAVAL ENSIGN

The swallow-tail form is common in Scandinavia for government flags.

THE PRESIDENT'S FLAG

The shield is supported by a bull, an eagle, a dragon, and a giant, the mythical defenders of the island.

Norway

Adopted July 13, 1821 | **Ratio** 8:11 | **Usage** National and Civil

The red, white, and blue colors were influenced by the French *Tricolore*—a symbol of liberty—and by the flags of the UK and US

Off-centered white cross on a red field is taken from the Danish flag

Ruled by Denmark from 1397, Norway passed to Sweden in 1814. It gained independence in 1905, when its union with Sweden was dissolved.

Until 1814, the Norwegian flag bore the Danish red and white cross. The current flag was born in 1821, during the period when Norway was united with Sweden. The flag combines two influences—its red and white coloring was taken from the Danish flag, and a blue cross was added overall. These three colors were chosen in honor of the French *Tricolore*, a symbol of revolution and liberty. They were also the colors of the flags of the United States of America and the United Kingdom, two other countries that were not ruled by an absolute monarch.

The Royal Standard consists of a banner of the Royal Arms, dating back to the Middle Ages. It depicts a lion rampant on a red field.

THE ROYAL STANDARD

The standard dates back to the Middle Ages

A tall, slender lion bearing the ax of St. Olav

Denmark

Adopted 1821 | **Ratio** 28:37 | **Usage** National and Civil

According to legend, a red flag with a white cross "appeared as a sign from heaven"

The off-centered cross is the basis for other Scandinavian countries' flags

Denmark is Europe's oldest kingdom, dating back to the 10th century. The present queen rules under a constitution granted in 1953.

Besides being the oldest monarchy in Europe, Denmark also has the oldest flag, known as the *Dannebrog*, or Danish cloth. Legend says that a bloodred flag with a white cross appeared as a sign from heaven to King Valdemar II during the conquest of Estonia in 1219. In reality, the flag may have been a gift from the Pope during the Crusades.

THE SCANDINAVIAN CROSS

The flag was originally square, but its design was elongated and the arm of the cross in the fly was extended. It has become a model for other flags.

OVERSEAS TERRITORIES

FAROE ISLANDS

The Faeroe Islands are a self-governing territory of Denmark.

The flag has the Norwegian colors in a new arrangement. This recalls that they were once part of Norway.

GREENLAND

Greenland's flag was designed by a local artist and adopted in 1985. In the Danish colors, white represents the ice that covers most of the island and red is for the Sun.

Sweden

Adopted June 22, 1906 | **Ratio** 5:8 | **Usage** National and Civil

The blue and yellow colors are taken from the national arms

The distinctive Scandinavian cross is taken from the flag of Denmark

Until 1523, when King Gustav Vasa laid the foundation of Sweden as a separate state, the country was under the influence of Denmark.

The present flag was adopted in 1906, but it was first used In a similar form almost four centuries before. The design is based on the Scandinavian cross. The flag's blue and yellow colors are thought to come from the national coat of arms—three gold crowns in a blue field—which originated in the 14th century. A national flag day is celebrated each year on June 6.

On this day in 1523 King Gustav Vasa was elected and, on the same date in 1809, Sweden adopted a new constitution.

SWEDISH ROYAL STANDARD
The coat of arms is placed in the center of the Royal Standard, which is used on special occasions by Parliament and dates from the 1440s.

THE ROYAL STANDARD

The shield is supported by two golden lions

The triple crown symbolizes the "Three Wise Men," a Swedish emblem since 1336

Finland

Adopted May 29, 1918 | **Ratio** 11:18 | **Usage** National and Civil

The overall design is based on the Scandinavian cross

Blue represents Finland's blue skies and its thousands of lakes

White recalls the snows of winter

Finland was part of Sweden starting in the 12th century. From 1809 until independence in 1917, it was part of the Russian Empire.

Like Sweden's, Finland's national flag is based on the Scandinavian cross.

It was adopted after independence from Russia, when many patriotic Finns wanted a special flag for their country, but its design dates back to the 19th century. The blue coloring is said to represent the country's thousands of lakes and the sky, with white for the snow that covers the land in winter.

This color combination has also been used over the centuries in various Finnish provincial, military, and town flags.

THE ÅLAND ISLANDS
The Åland Islands are an autonomous group of Finnish islands with their own flag since 1954. The design incorporates a Scandinavian cross.

THE FLAG OF THE ÅLAND ISLANDS

Red and yellow are taken from the arms of Finland, while blue and yellow represent Sweden; the islands have a large Swedish population

Estonia

Adopted May 8, 1990 | **Ratio** 7:11 | **Usage** National and Civil

Blue represents loyalty and Estonia's sky, sea, and lakes

Black is symbolic of past oppression and the soil

White represents virtue, the snow, and Estonia's struggle for freedom

Estonia declared independence from the Russian Empire in 1918. In 1940 it was annexed by the Soviet Union, but recovered its independence in 1991.

The tricolor was first adopted by students in 1881 during uprisings against occupying Russian Czarist forces. It was readopted as the national flag in 1990 just prior to independence. The colors represent Estonian history, folk costumes, and landscape. Blue is the color of loyalty and also represents the sky, sea, and lakes. Black symbolizes the past suffering of the people, the soil, and the traditional black peasant's jacket. White represents virtue and the struggle for freedom. It is also the color of birch bark and snow.

The great coat of arms was originally the emblem of a 13th-century Danish king.

GREAT ARMS OF ESTONIA

The shield is surrounded by golden branches of oak

Three blue leopards are ranged on a gold shield

Latvia

Adopted February 27, 1990 | **Ratio** 1:2 | **Usage** National and Civil

Red recalls the blood shed by the wounded leader

White may stand for the sheet used to wrap the wounded Latvian leader

Red also represents Latvians' willingness to defend their liberty

Over the centuries, Latvia has been invaded by Swedes, Poles, and Russians. It became independent from the Soviet Union in 1991.

Though officially adopted in 1922, the Latvian flag was in use from as early as the 13th century, but its use was suppressed during Soviet rule.

The red color has been described as symbolizing the readiness of the Latvians to give the blood from their hearts for freedom. An alternative interpretation, according to one legend, is that a Latvian leader was wounded in battle, and the edges of the white sheet in which he was wrapped were stained by his blood.

The coat of arms depicts a tripartite shield, recalling the three reunited duchies of Latvia. The shield is held by a red lion and a silver griffin.

ARMS OF LATVIA

Rising sun represents the Duchy of Latgale

The red lion represents the Duchy of Kurzeme

Three stars for the reunited duchies

The silver griffin recalls the Duchy of Vidzeme

Lithuania

Adopted March 20, 1989 | **Ratio** 3:5 | **Usage** National and Civil

Yellow represents wheat and freedom from want

Green symbolizes the forests and renewed hope

Red symbolizes patriotism and courage

After declaring independence from Russia in 1918, Lithuania was again occupied by the Soviet Union in 1940. It declared independence in 1991.

The national flag dates from the independent republic of 1918–40. It was suppressed under the Soviet regime, but was readopted in 1990. Yellow is said to stand for ripening wheat, green for the forests, and red for love of the country, or alternatively for the blood shed in defence of the nation. Red also refers to the color of the medieval banners of the kingdom of Lithuania. Together, the colors stand for hope, courage, and freedom from want.

ARMS OF LITHUANIA
The coat of arms' red shield dates from the 14th century. It was readopted in 1991.

ARMS OF LITHUANIA

A white knight on his charger

The double-barred cross commemorates the conversion of Grand Duke Jaggelon of Lithuania to Catholicism in 1386, at the time of his marriage to Queen Hedwig of Poland

Poland

Adopted August 1, 1919 | **Ratio** 5:8 | **Usage** National

The bicolor design was adopted after the First World War

White represents a desire for peace

In the past red was said to represent socialism

Poland is strategically placed in Europe and its borders have constantly shifted. They were last altered after the Second World War in 1945.

The red and white colors of the flag have been used since the 13th century, although they did not become the official national colors until 1831. They were taken from the colors of the national arms, first recorded in 1295.

THE NATIONAL ARMS

The coat of arms traditionally shows a white eagle on a red field. This emblem has remained more or less unchanged throughout Poland's turbulent history. The coat of arms was used by the Kingdom of Poland until its fall in 1795, and was readopted by the newly declared republic around 1918/19, when a zigzag border and crown were added. The border and the crown were both dropped under the communist administration, but the crown was restored in 1993.

THE PEOPLE'S REPUBLIC OF POLAND

Under communist rule from 1945–89, white was commonly said to represent the people's desire for peace, and during this period, red stood for socialism. The flag was reconfirmed as the national flag by the new government in 1992.

The plain bicolored flag is used for general purposes on land. When at sea, the flag is charged with the state arms in the center. Poland also has a swallow-tailed ensign, which is also charged with the state arms.

Germany

Adopted May 23, 1949 | **Ratio** 3:5 | **Usage** National and Civil

The colors of the German flag were taken from the uniforms of German soldiers during the Napoleonic Wars

First adopted in 1848, the flag was officially adopted for the republic in 1919

In 1919 the German Empire became a republic. In 1949 it was divided into East and West Germany, and in 1990 the two halves reunited.

Until the 19th century, Germany was a collection of feudal states. In 1848 an attempt was made to unite them, and although no union was established, a flag was produced. This was a black, red, and gold horizontal tricolor. The colors were taken from the uniforms of the German soldiers in the Napoleonic Wars in the late 18th century.

THE GERMAN EMPIRE

Most of the states finally united into the German Empire in 1871, but instead of retaining the black, red, and gold flag, the rival Bismarck tricolor of black, white, and red was adopted. This was a combination of the red of the Hanseatic League and the black and white of Prussia, of which Bismarck was Chancellor.

THE *WEIMAR* REPUBLIC

After Germany's defeat in the First World War a republic was declared in 1919 and the black, red, and gold flag returned. Its revival was short-lived and in 1933, when the Nazi government came to power, they restored the imperial colors and made their party flag, the *Hakenkreuz*, the national flag.

After the Second World War, both German states reverted to using the black, red, and gold tricolor, but East Germany added its coat of arms. Since reunification, the plain tricolor has been used.

Germany: Länder flags

On German regional flags, the arms only appear on the official versions (except Lower Saxony, Saarland, and Rhineland Palatinate).

Baden-Württemburg

The flag was adopted in 1953. Its colors derive from the arms of Duke Frederick V of Swabia; the coat of arms dates back to 1265. It was adopted as the state arms in 1954.

Bavaria

Bavaria's flag was adopted in 1950, but blue and white have been Bavarian colors since 1330, and the lozenge shapes first appeared on banners in the 15th century.

Berlin

The flag was first adopted for West Berlin in 1950 and extended to the whole city in 1991. The bear, a pun on the name Berlin, dates from 1338 and the colors from 1861.

Brandenburg

The colors of the flag are from the shield, dating from 1170, although red and white were also the colors of the medieval Hanseatic League. The flag was adopted in 1990.

Bremen

The flag of Bremen predates its coat of arms, which was adopted in 1891. Prior to this, Bremen was a member of the Hanseatic League, where the flag originated.

Hamburg

Used since 1325, red and white are the Hanseatic colors. The castle is for Hamburg; the three towers for the Trinity; the cross for Christ; the stars for the Father and Holy Spirit.

Hessen

The flag of Hessen was adopted in 1948. The coat of arms was that of Ludwig III of Thuringia in 1182. The red and white colors of the flag are taken from the lion in the arms.

Lower Saxony

This flag uses the national flag with Lower Saxony's local arms in the center. It was adopted in 1946, but the arms dates from 1361, when it appeared on the seal of the ruler.

Länder flags (continued)

Mecklenburg-Vorpommern

This flag, adopted in 1991, combines blue and white of Pomerania with the blue, yellow, and red of Mecklenburg. The bull and the griffin are also local emblems. Red and white recall the Hanseatic League.

North-Rhine-Westphalia

The coat of arms depicts the River Rhine of the Rhineland, the horse of Westphalia, and the rose of Lippe: the three territories that united to form the state. The colors of the flag are from the arms.

Rhineland-Palatinate

The flag was adopted in 1948 when the arms were placed on the national flag. The coat of arms depicts the lion of the Palatinate dating from 1229, the cross of Trier from 1273, and the wheel of Mainz from 1335.

Saarland

Adopted in 1957, the flag of Saarland recalls the different parts of the state. Depicted on the shield is the lion of Saarbrücken, the cross of Trier, the eagles of Lorraine, and the lion of Pfalz-Zweibrücken.

Saxony

The flag was adopted in 1991, but the coat of arms is the traditional symbol of the rulers of Saxony: black and yellow bands and the green crown of rue. The white and green flag dates from the 19th century.

Saxony-Anhalt

This flag was the same as Baden-Württemberg until 1991, when the colors were reversed. The eagle recalls Prussi; the bicolored bands and rue crown, Saxony; and the bear and wall are the arms of Anhalt.

Schleswig-Holstein

The shield depicts two lions from the arms of Schleswig and a nettle leaf from those of Holstein. The colors of the flag, adopted in 1957, are taken from the arms.

Thuringia

Another flag whose colors are based on the state arms, it was adopted in 1991. The red and white lion was the arms of the Counts of Thuringia in the 12th century.

The Netherlands

Adopted February 19, 1937 | **Ratio** 2:3 | **Usage** National and Civil

In the mid-17th century, red, rather than orange, was made the official color

Blue and white originally represented faith in God

Independent from Spain in the 16th century, the Netherlands was a republic until the Napoleonic Wars, and became a kingdom in 1814.

The first *stadtholder*, or ruler, of the Dutch Republic was William of Orange, who joined with Dutch nationalists and led the struggle for independence from Spain.

THE PRINSVLAG
Partly out of respect for him, the first flag adopted by the Dutch, was a horizontal tricolor of orange, white, and blue (see p.20). It became known as the *Prinsenvlag* and was based on the livery of William of Orange. The orange dye was particularly unstable and tended to turn red after a while, so in the mid-17th century, red was made the official color. The flag has flown since then, but was only confirmed by

Royal Decree in 1937. As the first revolutionary flag, it has had a seminal influence throughout the world, particularly on the Pan-Slavic colors of Russia.

Until about 1800, in the case of both the orange- and red-striped versions, the number of stripes and their order frequently varied.

ARMS OF THE NETHERLANDS
The Dutch coat of arms depicts a golden lion on a blue shield, holding a sword and a sheaf of arrows. It is a combination of the coat of arms of the Dutch Republic and that of the House of Orange. The seven arrows represent the seven original provinces in the Netherlands.

Provincial flags

Except for South Holland and North Brabant, all the Dutch provincial flags are modern creations.

Drenthe

White and red are the colors of the Archbishops of Utrecht, former rulers of Drenthe. The black castle and stars recall the uprising of Coevorden against the archbishop.

Flevoland

Blue is for the Lake Ijssel from which the province was reclaimed. Green is for vegetation, and yellow for the cornfields. The lily recalls Lely, the engineer of the reclamation project.

Friesland

The flag is based on that of the 15th-century kings of Friesland. The colors are those of the Dutch flag. The stripes and pompbleden (the leaves of the yellow water lily) represent the seven districts of Friesland.

Gelderland

In 1371, the dukedoms of Gelre and Gulik were united and combined their arms. The new arms was blue, yellow, and black. These colors also appear in the flag, which was hoisted in 1953.

Groningen

The flag, adopted in 1950, combines green and white from the town of Groningen, surrounded by red, white, and blue of Ommeland, reflecting the town's position.

Provincial flags (continued)

Limburg

The red lion is from Limburg's arms. White and yellow are from local coats of arms, while the narrow blue stripe is for the Maas River which crosses the province.

North Brabant

The design, adopted in 1959, originated in Antwerp where red and white checked coats of arms were popular. It was associated with the area from the 17th century.

North Holland

Adopted in 1958, this flag unites the colors of Holland—yellow and red— with the blue and yellow of West Friesland. Yellow, the common color, is placed at the top.

Overijssel

The yellow and red stripes recall the ancient association of the province with Holland. The wavy blue stripe running across the center is for the Ijssel River, after which the province is named.

South Holland

The flag is a banner of the arms of Holland and was adopted in this form in 1986, replacing the previous simple triband of yellow-red-yellow, which was also based on the colors of the arms.

Provincial/Overseas Territory flags

Utrecht

The Archbishop of Utrecht used a red flag with a white cross from 1528. The Archbishop's flag remains in the canton of the modern flag, adopted in 1952. The field is in the traditional colors of the province.

Zeeland

The flag of Zeeland, adopted in 1949, shows its full coat of arms. The wavy blue and white stripes represent the sea and the constant struggle to control it. From the water, the Dutch lion rises in triumph.

Aruba

The flag of Aruba was adopted in 1976 when it was still administered as part of the Netherlands Antilles. The flag was retained when Aruba became autonomous in 1986.

Curaçao

Curaçao's flag was adopted in 1984, designed by Martin Den Dulk. The blue symbolizes the sky and sea, and the yellow stripe, the sunshine that bathes the island. The two stars represent Curaçao and Klein Curaçao.

Bonaire

The flag of Bonaire, adopted in 1984, consists of yellow and blue triangles which represent the sun and the sea, while the white represents the sky. The six-pointed red star represents the six original villages that made up the territory.

Sint Maarten

Introduced in 1985, the Sint Maarten flag has two horizontal bands of red and blue, with a white triangle, representing its past association with the Netherlands and France. Its coat of arms depicts the distinctive courthouse in Philipsburg, the capital.

Belgium

Adopted January 23, 1831 | **Ratio** 13:15 | **Usage** National and Civil

Black is taken from the shield of the arms

Red is adapted from the lion's claws and tongue

Gold is the color of the lion in the arms

Following centuries of foreign domination, Belgium finally gained international recognition as an independent kingdom in 1830.

The Belgian colors black, yellow, and red derive from the arms of Brabant, a black shield with a gold lion having red tongue and claws. The first flag in these colors, but with horizontal stripes, appeared in 1792 in a revolt against Austrian rule. Upon gaining independence in 1831, they were changed to vertical in imitation of the French *Tricolore*.

BELGIAN REGIONAL FLAGS

Brussels

Adopted in 1991, the lily was widespread in the area that later became Brussels.

German region

Adopted in 1990, the lion recalls former owner, Limburg; nine roses are for the nine communes.

Flanders

Adopted in 1985, it is based on the arms, and the colors are taken from the national flag.

Wallonia

The cockerel is derived from the Gallic rooster, recalling the cultural links with France.

Ireland

Adopted January 21, 1919 | **Ratio** 1:2 | **Usage** National and Civil

Green represents the Catholic people

White is for the union between Catholics and Protestants

Orange is for the Protestant people

After centuries of British rule, Ireland was split in 1921, becoming the Free State (The Republic of Ireland) and the northern Six Counties.

The Irish flag is modeled on that of the French *Tricolore*. It was first flown by nationalists during their struggle for freedom from Britain in 1848, a year of Europe-wide revolution. However, it was not until the Easter Rising of 1916 that it came to be regarded as the national flag. It was officially confirmed in 1919 and was written into the Constitution in 1937. The green coloring on the flag represents the Catholic majority; orange is for the Protestant minority (originally supporters of William of Orange), and white is for peace between the two faiths.

THE PRESIDENT'S STANDARD

The flag of the president was introduced in 1945 and is based on the ancient "Green Flag," a traditional symbol of Irish nationalism.

THE PRESIDENT'S STANDARD

The harp is said to be the harp of Brian Boru, an 11th-century ruler

The flag is similar to the quartering for Ireland on the Royal Arms of the United Kingdom

United Kingdom

Adopted January 1, 1801 | **Ratio** 1:2 | **Usage** National and Civil

The saltire of St. Patrick has been counterchanged with the white saltire of St. Andrew

The white saltire on a blue field was taken from the St. Andrew's Cross

The central red cross, fimbriated with white, was adapted from the St. George's Cross

The United Kingdom was formed in 1707, uniting England, Scotland, and Wales. In 1801, Ireland joined, but in 1921, the south broke away.

The Union Flag is probably one of the world's best known flags, partially due to its unusual design, but more important, because of the significance of the British Empire in world history.

THE FIRST UNION FLAG

When King James of Scotland became King of England in 1603, both countries retained their own flags. Even today, the St. George's Cross and St. Andrew's Cross remain the flags of England and Scotland, respectively. In 1606, King James considered it necessary to have a flag reflecting the new union of Scotland and England, and ordered that a Union Flag, more commonly known as the Union Jack, be flown on British ships, combining the English Cross of St. George with the Scottish Cross of St. Andrew.

A NEW UNION FLAG

In 1801, when Ireland joined the Union, the so-called Cross of St. Patrick was added to form the present flag, but was counterchanged with the Cross of St. Andrew.

A ROYAL FLAG

The Union Flag was established as a maritime flag and it remains a royal flag, not officially a national flag. In 1915, King George V gave permission for British citizens to use the flag on land.

UK: Subnational flags

Most regional flags are older than the Union Flag, except those based on the St. George's Cross, which date from the 20th century.

England

Originally used in 1191, the flag of St. George became the flag of England after 1277. The white flag has a red upright cross throughout. At sea it is the flag of an Admiral.

Scotland (National flag)

In use since 1512, the Scottish flag is the Cross of St. Andrew. As James was King of Scotland before he was King of England, this flag formed the basis of the Union Flag.

Wales

Approved in 1959 as the Welsh national flag, the Red Dragon is an ancient emblem of Wales. For a time it appeared on a green hill, but the horizontal division is traditional.

State flags

Scotland (The Standard) Territory

The red lion on gold is the traditional royal flag of Scotland. The *fleur-de-lis* on the border recall the "auld alliance" with France. Its exact date of adoption is not known.

Guernsey

Guernsey formerly used only the Cross of St. George. In 1985, a gold cross taken from the flag of William the Conqueror at the Battle of Hastings was added to the flag.

Isle of Man

This is a traditional design, which was adopted in 1968. The *Trinacria*, three legs of Man, has been used for several centuries in varying forms, but its origin is uncertain.

Jersey

Prior to the adoption of its current flag, Jersey used a red diagonal cross on white, which is the same as the saltire of St. Patrick. The arms were added in 1981.

Royal Standards

Like other monarchies, the UK has a wide range of flags which are armorial or semi-armorial, for the leading members of its royal family. In the case of HM Queen, it is necessary to distinguish between her role as Queen of the United Kingdom and her other Realms, and as Head of the Commonwealth. In addition to her British Royal Standard, she has standards for other Realms.

Royal Standard of the United Kingdom

This form has been in use since the accession of Queen Victoria in 1837 and depicts the three areas united to form the United Kingdom (England, Scotland, and Northern Ireland). Strictly, flags of this kind are armorial banners rather than "standards."

Queen as Head of the Commonwealth

This is used when the Queen is not in a "Queen's Realm" (i.e. a country of which she is directly the Head of State) or in one which does not have a local Royal Standard. It is a banner with Her Majesty's initial "E," a gold crown, and chaplet of roses.

Prince Philip Duke of Edinburgh

The banner for Prince Philip has quarters representing his descent from the royal families of both Denmark and Greece, and from the Mountbattens. His title Duke of Edinburgh is represented by the arms of the city.

Royal Standards (continued)

HRH Prince Charles Prince of Wales

The banner is an adaptation of the Royal Standard, with a "label" for the eldest son: a white bar with three points, and the quartered arms of the Principality of Wales in the center. Labels are used for children and grandchildren of the Queen.

HRH Prince Charles for use in Wales

For personal visits to Wales and as his own flag, the Prince uses the banner of the Principality of Wales with his crown on a green shield over all in the center. The Prince also has banners for his titles in Cornwall, Rothesay, and as Lord of the Isles.

Other Royal Standards

Other members of the Queen's family who have standards based on the Royal Standard are the Princess Royal, the Duke of York, Earl of Wessex, and the Queen's royal cousins. There is a general banner for those members of the royal family not entitled to an individual standard.

Overseas territories

Official flags for British Overseas Territories are generally based on the British blue or government ensign with a local badge in the fly.

Anguilla

The flag of Anguilla was adopted in 1990. It is a blue ensign with the badge of the island. This derives from the unofficial flag used locally on land only.

Anguilla (Unofficial)

Adopted in 1967, when the island separated from neighboring St. Kitts and Nevis. The turquoise stripe represents the sea, and the three dolphins are for friendship, wisdom, and strength.

Bermuda

Unusually, Bermuda uses a red ensign. The badge shows a lion holding a shield on which appears the 1609 wreck of a ship, which struck a reef, not a cliff as is shown.

British Virgin Islands

The badge dates from 1909, and the flag from 1956. It shows St. Ursula, the namesake of the islands, with a lamp. She was martyred with 11,000 virgins, which are represented by 11 lamps.

Overseas territories (continued)

British Antarctic Territory

The white field of the new flag, approved in 1998, symbolizes the snow which covers the Antarctic continent. It is used by research stations within the territory.

British Indian Ocean Territory

The flag was adopted in 1990. Blue and white wavy lines represent the ocean, and the palm recalls the natural vegetation of the islands. The crown shows British possession of the territory.

Cayman Islands

Blue and white lines recall the sea and the three stars, the three main islands. The lion of England appears above: the crest is a turtle, and a pineapple is representative of the fauna and flora.

Falkland Islands

The badge shows a ram for the sheep industry of the islands. The ship is the *Desire*, the ship of John Davies who discovered the islands in 1592. The flag was hoisted in 1948.

Tristan da Cunha

The flag was adopted in 2002. It shows a stylistic image of the main island in the sea surrounded by four albatrosses. The arms show a Tristan longboat above a Naval Crown, with a central shield decorated with four albatrosses. The supporters are Tristan lobsters, the island's main export.

Gibraltar (City)

The local flag of Gibraltar City is a banner of the arms officially granted in 1926. It is based on the original arms granted by Spain in 1502. The banner was granted for use exclusively on land in 1983. Like the badge, it depicts a red fortress with a gold key. The red and white field is derived from the arms.

Montserrat

The coat of arms dates from 1909, although its origin is unknown. It shows a woman in green holding a cross and a harp. The cross is for Christianity, and the woman and harp recall Irish immigrants who settled on the island in 1632. The arms was readopted in 1962, when the West Indies Federation was dissolved.

Overseas territories (continued)

Pitcairn Islands

Adopted for the Pitcairn Islands in 1984, the badge commemorates the island's earliest settlers, the infamous crew of *HMS Bounty*, who mutinied in 1790. The badge is blue to represent the Pacific Ocean, with a green triangle symbolizing the island. The shield is charged with the Bible and the anchor of *HMS Bounty*.

St. Helena

The current badge was made into a coat of arms in 1984. It depicts a ship flying the Cross of St. George sailing between two cliffs. Above is a wirebird representing the local fauna. The flag is also flown in the Ascension Islands and Tristan da Cunha, dependencies administered by St. Helena.

Turks and Caicos Islands

The blue ensign was granted in 1968, three years after the arms. The shield from the arms shows a conch shell and a crayfish representing fishing (the islands' main industry) and a cactus for their flora. The Turks and Caicos became a separate colony after the Bahamas achieved independence.

Military flags

Royal Navy 1864

The flag incorporates the cross of St. George and includes the Union Jack in the canton. It is flown by the British Navy, and is also used by the Royal Yacht Squadron and by ships escorting the reigning British monarch.

Royal Air Force 1921

The Blue Ensign bears the Royal Air Force roundel in the middle of the fly. The flag is hoisted from the flagpole of every Royal Air Force station during daylight hours, and is on permanent display at the Cenotaph in London.

British Army 1938

The Union Jack is the British Army's official flag, but this non-ceremonial version bearing the Monarch's insignia is used at military events and exhibitions. Sometimes the word "army" appears below the badge.

Royal Fleet Auxiliary 1864

The Royal Fleet Auxiliary is an amalgam of the supply and support vessels that provide logistical assistance to the Royal Navy. Its flag uses the Blue Ensign with the symbol of an anchor in the middle of the fly.

France

Adopted February 15, 1794 | **Ratio** 2:3 | **Usage** National and Civil

Blue, white, and red have come to represent liberty, equality, and fraternity—the ideals of the French Revolution

Red and blue are the colors of Paris

White is the color of the House of Bourbon

France was a monarchy until the the Revolution of 1789. A republic was created in 1792, following the abolition of the monarchy.

The traditional emblem of France was the *fleur-de-lis*, or lily, which first appeared on the arms in the 12th century.

The *Tricolore* was used during the Revolution, and has since become a symbol of liberty around the world. Other nations have also adopted the design. Because France has no arms, the *Tricolore* is also the national emblem.

The colors are probably derived from those of Paris, combined with those of the Bourbon Dynasty, though they are usually associated with liberty, equality, and fraternity.

OVERSEAS TERRITORIES

ST. PIERRE & MIQUELON

These islands lie just south of Canada's Newfoundland. The flag features the emblems of the Basques, Bretons, and Normans who settled the islands.

FRENCH POLYNESIA

Red and white are local colors. The emblem depicts a *pirogue*—a local canoe—below a rising sun. The five crew members recall the five island groups.

Luxembourg

Adopted 1848 | **Ratio** 3:5 | **Usage** National

The colors date back to the 13th century

The blue stripe is paler than that of the Netherlands

For most of the 19th century Luxembourg was part of the Netherlands. It gained independence in 1890 and is Europe's last independent duchy.

Luxembourg had no flag until 1830, when patriots were urged to display the national colors. The flag was defined as a horizontal tricolor of red, white, and blue in 1848, but it was not officially adopted until 1972. The tricolor flag is almost identical to that of the Netherlands, except that it is longer, and its blue stripe is a lighter shade. The red, white, and blue coloring was derived from the Grand Duke's coal of arms, which dates from the 13th century.

THE CIVIL ENSIGN
Since 1972 a banner of the Grand Duke's arms has been used as a civil ensign for use at sea. This is a blue-and-white striped field with a lion rampant in the center.

LUXEMBOURG CIVIL ENSIGN

Red, white, and blue coloring gave rise to colors of national flag

A crowned two-tailed rampant lion

Monaco

Adopted April 4, 1881 | **Ratio** 4:5 | **Usage** National and Civil

The bicolor design is common on other national flags, such as San Marino; it is often used as a background for heraldic livery

Red and white are the heraldic colors of the Grimaldi family

The Grimaldis, a Genoese family, have ruled Monaco since the 13th century. Until 1860, the principality was considered part of Italy.

The present bicolor design was adopted in 1881 under Prince Charles III. It is identical to the far younger Indonesian national flag except in its statutory proportions, which are 4:5, compared to 2:3.

The Grimaldi coat of arms, which appears on the state flag, is the traditional one of the princely family and consists of a shield supported by two monks bearing swords. The device alludes to the legend of 1297, in which the Grimaldis conquered Monaco after entering the city with soldiers disguised as monks. Earlier Monegasque flags incorporated the Grimaldi shield and crown on a white field.

ARMS OF GRIMALDIS

A princely crown

The Grimaldi motto—"*Deo Juvante*" ("With God's Help")

The collar of the Order of St. Charles surrounds a shield of red and white (or silver)

Andorra

Adopted August 27, 1971 | **Ratio** 7:10 | **Usage** National and Civil

The colors reflect Andorra's dependence upon France and Spain for its national security

Red and blue taken from the colors of France

Red and yellow are taken from the colors of Spain

Andorran coat of arms

The Principality of Andorra is an independent republic in the Pyrenees, between France and Spain. It is one of the world's oldest states.

The principality of Andorra has been under Franco-Spanish protection since 1278, governed by the Counts of Foix and the Bishops of Urgel. The colors of its national flag reflect both France (blue and red) and Spain (yellow and red). The Andorran coat of arms is placed in the middle of the yellow stripe.

ARMS OF ANDORRA

Like the colors of the flag, the coat of arms also depicts the areas on which Andorra has been dependent. The quartered shield represents Urgel by the crozier and miter, Foix by the three vertical red stripes, Catalonia by the four vertical red stripes, and Béarn by the two cows.

ARMS OF ANDORRA

The crozier and miter symbolize the Bishops of Urgel

The four red stripes are taken from the arms of Catalonia

The three red stripes recall the Counts of Foix

The two cows are taken from the arms of Béarn

The motto is, "*Virtus Unita Fortior*"—"Strength united is stronger"

Portugal

Adopted June 30, 1911 | **Ratio** 2:3 | **Usage** National and Civil

Green represents a Portuguese explorer: King Henry the Navigator

The armillary sphere—an early navigational tool

Red represents revolution

During the 15th and 16th centuries, Portugal played a leading role in discovering the world beyond Europe. It formed a republic in 1910.

The present flag with red for revolution and green for Portuguese exploration dates from 1910. The central emblem is an armillary sphere, an early navigational instrument, on which is the former royal arms of Portugal. The white shield was first used by King Sancho I. The five blue shields recall the victory of King Afonso Henriques over five Muslim princes. The red edge and castles are representative of the marriage of King Alfonso III to a Spanish princess in 1252.

EMBLEM OF PORTUGAL

Five blue shields recall the victory of King Afonso Henriques

Gold castles on red recall the marriage of King Alfonso III to a Spanish Princess

This armillary sphere and shields appear in the center of the Portuguese coat of arms

The armillary sphere recalls the importance of Portuguese exploration of the globe

Spain

Adopted July 19, 1927 | **Ratio** 2:3 | **Usage** National and Civil

Red and yellow are the colors of the arms of both Castille and Aragón

The first red and yellow flag of Spain was adopted in the 18th century for use at sea

The present layout was adopted in 1927

Spain was united in the 15th century and rapidly became an imperial power. It lost most of its colonies during the 19th century.

Early Spanish flags were mostly heraldic; some, like the flag of Castilla y León (see p.194), survive today.

In 1785 the King of Spain adopted red and yellow, a bold combination of colors then used by no other country, to distinguish Spanish ships. The present pattern was finally established in 1927.

THE SPANISH REPUBLIC

When Spain became a republic in 1931, an equal horizontal tricolor in red, yellow, and purple became the new flag. Purple was from the arms of León. At the end of the Spanish Civil War (1936–39) the original flag was restored.

The state flag has the national arms set toward the hoist.

ARMS OF SPAIN

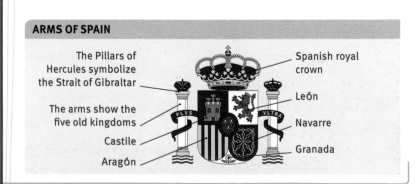

The Pillars of Hercules symbolize the Strait of Gibraltar

The arms show the five old kingdoms

Castile

Aragón

Spanish royal crown

León

Navarre

Granada

Spain: Regional flags

Although most of the flags were adopted recently, all are based on older models, or traditional arms, reflecting continuity with the past.

Andalusia

Adopted in 1918, but not confirmed until 1983, the colors were those used during the Napoleonic Wars. The coat of arms depicts the Pillars of Hercules and the lions of Cadiz.

Aragón

The stripes of Aragón date from the 14th century. Tradition states that a King of Aragón drew bloodstained fingers over a gold shield. The flag was adopted in 1981.

Asturias

Blue is the color of the Virgin Mary. The cross is the Cross of Victory, a traditional Asturian emblem. From it hang Greek letters, symbolizing Christ, the Beginning, and the End.

Baleares

The field is the same as the flag of Aragón, to which the islands belonged in medieval times. The canton is the emblem of Palma de Majorca, the islands' capital.

The Basque Country (País Vasco)

This flag was first adopted in 1931 and readopted in 1979. It is based on the Union Jack. Red recalls bloodshed, white the Catholic faith, and green the Oak of Guérnica.

Canary Islands (Islas Canarias)

The colors symbolize those of the Virgin Mary and the Papacy. They are also thought to evoke the blue sea, the white beaches, and the golden sun. It was adopted in 1989.

Cantabria

White and red are the traditional colors of the area. The arms allude to the seafaring customs of the people and include an ancient seal. The flag was adopted in 1981.

Castilla-la Mancha

Adopted in 1989, the deep red stripe and the castle are the emblem of Castile. The white panel is intended to recall the surcoats worn by the soldiers in the Crusades.

Regional flags (continued)

Castilla y León

This flag has been used by Castilla y León since 1248. It depicts the union of Castilla (castle) and León (lion). It was adopted for the region in 1989.

Catalonia (Catalunya)

The flag, adopted in 1932, has been used since the 13th century and has the same origin as that of Aragón. It was outlawed from 1939 to 1975.

Extremadura

This flag was adopted in 1985, but the colors are traditional regional colors. Green is for fidelity, white for truth, and black for courage.

Galicia

Based on a traditional Galician design, white and blue are the colors of the Virgin Mary. The arms reflects loyalty to the Catholic Church.

La Rioja

The upper red stripe was originally to be in the color of Rioja wine, but is now simply red. The colors are taken from the arms.

Madrid

The flag, adopted in 1983, is in the traditional color of Castilla. The seven white stars, from the arms, represent the seven districts of the region.

Murcia

The four castles recall Murcia's links with Castilla: the seven crowns, the seven regions of the province.

Navarre

The red field and golden chains of Navarre date from the 14th century. The current flag was adopted in 1982.

Valencia

The stripes recall Valencia's links with Catalonia. The blue decorative band on the hoist side is representative of its own unique identity.

Italy

Adopted January 1, 1948 | **Ratio** 2:3 | **Usage** National

Green was said to be Napoleon's favorite color

The first vertical tricolor was used until 1814, and was readopted in 1861

Italy was a collection of city states, dukedoms, and monarchies before it became a unified nation in 1861. Italy became a republic in 1946.

The Italian tricolor comes from the standard designed by Napoleon during the Italian campaign of 1796. The coloring was influenced by the French *Tricolore*, at first appearing in horizontal bands. The vertical tricolor was introduced in 1798, but was only used until 1814. It was reintroduced when the new Kingdom of Italy was formed in 1861.

When the monarchy ended in 1946, the coat of arms of the House of Savoy was removed from the flag. The present flag was officially adopted in 1946.

ITALIAN CIVIL ENSIGN
The most famous seafaring states of ancient Italy are commemorated in the quarters of the civil ensign.

ITALIAN CIVIL ENSIGN

The winged lion of St. Mark represents Venice

The Maltese cross recalls Amalfi

The Cross of St. George represents Genoa

The Pisan cross stands for Pisa

Malta

Adopted September 21, 1964 | **Ratio** 2:3 | **Usage** National

The George Cross is fimbriated with red

Red and white were adapted from the badge of the Knights of Malta

Malta was ruled successively by the Knights of St. John of Jerusalem, by Napoleon, and by Britain. It became independent in 1964.

A key stronghold during the Crusades, much of the heraldry of Malta is influenced by the colors and devices of the Knights of Malta. Their badge was the characteristic Maltese cross and their arms was a white cross on a red field. From these colors came the red and white shield that was used during the colonial period. The George Cross medal was added to the shield in 1943. It was awarded to the islanders by King George VI of Britain for heroism in World War II. In 1964, the blue canton on which the cross was originally placed was replaced by a red fimbriation.

The president's flag, introduced in 1988, has the shield on a blue field with a Maltese cross in each corner.

THE PRESIDENT'S FLAG

The wreath of olive and palm branches represents peace

A gold mural crown with a sally port and eight turrets represents fortifications of Valetta

The Maltese cross

The Shield of Malta

Vatican City

Adopted June 7, 1929 | **Ratio** 1:1 | **Usage** Civil

Yellow (gold) and white (iron) are the colors of St. Peter's keys

The emblem features St. Peter's keys supporting the papal crown

White and yellow were adopted as the papal colors in 1808

Vatican City, the Holy See of the Roman Catholic Church, is the smallest independent state in the world.

The modern Vatican colors were first adopted as the papal colors in 1808. The flag was used until 1870 when the Papal States were incorporated into a new unified Italy. In 1929, the Papal States were granted independent status, but their authority was confined to Vatican City. Gold and iron, represented in the flag as yellow and white, are the colors of the keys of St. Peter, which have accompanied papal arms since the Middle Ages. The flag's white stripe bears an emblem used since the 13th century to represent the Vatican's role as the headquarters of the Roman Catholic Church.

EMBLEM OF VATICAN CITY

The crossed keys represent the keys to the Kingdom of Heaven bestowed by Christ on St. Peter

The triple crown signifies the three types of temporal power—legislative, executive, and judicial—vested in the Pope

A red rope binds the keys

San Marino

Adopted April 6, 1862 | **Ratio** 3:4 | **Usage** National and Civil

The colors are taken from the traditional arms, which is placed at the center of the flag for official purposes only

White represents the snow on Mt. Titano and the clouds above it

Blue recalls the sky

Founded in the 4th century, the Republic of San Marino is one of the smallest and oldest in the world. It lies on the slopes of Mt. Titano in Italy.

The flag of San Marino dates back to 1797 and was recognized by Napoleon as that of an independent state in 1799. The colors were taken from the coat of arms and were introduced in the 18th century. Blue is said to represent the sky over San Marino, and white the clouds and snow on Mt. Titano. The traditional coat of arms is placed in the center of the flag for official purposes only. It depicts three white towers crowned with ostrich plumes, representing three citadels resting on the peak of Mt. Titano, which was once vaned with ostrich feathers. They symbolize the state's ability to defend itself.

ARMS OF SAN MARINO

A laurel wreath

The motto *"Libertas,"* meaning "Liberty", also dates back to the 4th century, when the state was established as a refuge for those fleeing religious persecution

A wreath of oak

The towers represent the three citadels, Guaita, Cesta, and Montale, situated on Mt. Titano

Switzerland

Adopted December 12, 1889 | **Ratio** 1:1 | **Usage** National and Civil

The red field with a white cross was adapted from the flag of Schwyz, one of the original three cantons

The Swiss and Vatican flags are the only square national flags

A white coupled cross

In 1291, a small confederation was formed to resist Austrian rule, beginning modern Switzerland. More cantons joined up to 1815.

The flag of Switzerland is one of the most typical European flags. In the medieval era, many European states used a plain flag with a cross.

A FLAG FOR THE CONFEDERATION

For many years, the separate cantons of Switzerland had no one common flag, but were each represented by its own flag. The present flag of Switzerland, a white coupled cross on a red field, was based on that of Schwyz, one of the three original provinces that united into a confederation against the Holy Roman Empire in 1291. It became accepted as the common badge of the Confederation in 1339 at the Battle of Laupen, when it was used to distinguish the soldiers of

the Confederation from other soldiers, and became the accepted flag of the Confederation in 1480. It was not officially confirmed as the flag of Switzerland until 1848, and it was last regulated in 1889.

Apart from that of the Vatican, the Swiss flag is the only totally square national flag. However, when used on the Swiss lakes it has the ratio of 2:3—a practice adopted in 1941.

THE NATIONAL ARMS

The coat of arms is simply a shield in the form of the flag. It was officially adopted in 1889. Every town or commune in Switzerland has its own flag and coat of arms.

Switzerland: Canton flags

In every case the flags are based on the arms of the canton,
some of which predate the canton's joining the Swiss Confederation.

Aargau

Adopted in 1803, the white waves on black
represent the River Aare, and the white stars
on blue, the districts of Baden, the Free
Areas, and Fricktal, which came together to
form the canton. In 1963, it was decreed that
the stars should be arranged two on top and
one below.

Appenzell Ausser-Rhoden

Adopted in 1597, when the canton separated
from the Inner-Rhoden, the flag retained
the bear, but added the initials VR (for
Ussroden). The bear dates back to medieval
banners. It was used from 1403 in battles
against feudal landlords.

Appenzell Inner-Rhoden

This is the original form of the flag before
the partition from Appenzell Ausser-Rhoden
in 1597. The bear emblem was widely used
locally in the Middle Ages, and was taken by
the Appenzellers from the arms of the abbey
of Sankt Gallen.

Basel-Land

Basel-Land separated from the City in
1832. The arms and flag were adopted in
1834, based on the form of crosier used
in Liestal, with the crook turned to the
right and decorated with small spheres.
This was made official in 1947.

Canton flags (continued)

Basel-Stadt

The emblem of Basel-Stadt is the headpiece of a bishop's crosier. The emblem dates back to the earliest days of heraldry. Since the 15th century it has been depicted as black on white. It was kept in this form when the canton was divided in 1832.

Bern

The coat of arms dates back to the 12th century. Soon after, the arms, which depict a bear on a red field with a yellow diagonal, became the canton's banner. There have, however, been many variant forms through the ages. The bear represents the name of the canton.

Fribourg

The original colors of Fribourg, black and white, were readopted when it joined the Confederation in 1831, but the colors actually date back to 1410 and are related to the coat of arms.

Geneva

The eagle recalls the former Holy Roman Empire. The key is the Key of St. Peter, and shows Geneva as the key to western Switzerland. The flag was adopted in 1815.

Glarus

The flag of Glarus depicts the figure of St. Fridolin, the patron saint of the canton, on a red field. The flag was adopted when the canton joined the Confederation in 1352.

Graubunden

The flag includes symbols for the three original parts of the canton which united in the 15th century: Graubunden, Zehgerichtenbund, and the Gotteshausbund.

Jura

This flag was adopted 1978, when Jura became a separate canton. It was formerly part of Basel-Land—recalled by the crosier—and Bern. The stripes are from the arms of Jura.

Lucerne

Lucerne was the first canton, after the original three, to join the Confederation in 1332. Its flag has the colors of its shield arranged horizontally instead of vertically.

Canton flags (continued)

Neuchâtel

The tricolor adopted in 1848 is in traditional colors. The white cross was added to show the canton's association with Switzerland.

Nidwalden

The key with two wards is the emblem of St. Peter, and was used in the 15th century. It was retained when the canton divided in 1815.

Obwalden

The red and white flag was used in Obwalden from the 13th century, and it was adopted when the separate canton was formed in 1815. Moreover, a key was added in 1816.

Sankt Gallen

The emblems of Sankt Gallen—an ax and a fasces—were adopted in 1803 when the canton was formed under French influence. They are both symbols of republicanism.

Schaffhausen

The emblem has been in use since the 14th century. It depicts a ram (the "sheep" of the town's name) on a yellow field. The flag's existence was first recorded as early as 1386.

Schwyz

Schwyz was one of the first three cantons, and the one from which the country takes its name. Its arms existed before the Confederation was formed in 1291.

Solothurn

The coat of arms dates back to 1394 and has colors derived from those of the Confederation. The flag was originally red with a white cross, but was simplified into its current form.

Thurgau

The flag of Thurgau, adopted in 1803, depicts two gold lions arranged diagonally. They are taken from the coat of arms, which dates from the medieval era.

Ticino

The colors of Ticino's flag may be derived from the French *Tricolore*, or from the main colors of the arms of the united townships.

Uri

The emblem is an auroch's head (linked to the canton's name). It dates from the 13th century, but the nose ring was added later.

Canton flags (continued)

Valais

The modern flag of Valais is derived from that of the original republic, which had seven stars for its component townships. These were increased to 12 in 1802 and retained when the state joined the Confederation in 1814.

Vaud

The colors date from 1798 when the Léman Republic was formed, and stand for freedom. They were retained when the state entered the Confederation in 1803. The motto is *"Liberté et Patrie"* ("Freedom and Fatherland").

Zug

Zug joined the Confederation in 1352 and again in 1364, after a brief return to Habsburg rule. The colors of the flag were originally red-white-red of Austria, but were altered to the blue and white from the arms of the Counts of Lenzburg in 1352.

Zürich

The flag in this case preceded the arms and dates back to the 13th century. It was adopted in 1351 when Zürich joined the Confederation. However, since 1957, it has been compulsory to depict the flag in the same format as the shield.

Liechtenstein

Adopted June 24, 1937 | **Ratio** 3:5 | **Usage** National and Civil

The yellow crown was introduced to distinguish Liechtenstein as a principality

Royal blue and red have been used to represent the country of Liechtenstein since the 18th century

The Principality of Liechtenstein was created in 1719 as part of the Holy Roman Empire. It gained full independence in 1806.

The red and blue of Liechtenstein's flag date from 1921. There was confusion at the 1936 Olympic Games in Berlin because the flag was very similar to that of Haiti. In 1937 the crown was introduced to the flag of Liechtenstein to establish the country's status as a principality and to distinguish it from the Haitian flag. The flag can be hung vertically or horizontally, but the crown always remains upright.

THE PRINCE'S FLAG
The arms of Silesia, Künringen, Troppau, and East Friesland and Rietburg make up the four quarters of the shield of the Prince's arms, in the center of his flag. They represent the noble ancestors of the prince.

THE FLAG OF PRINCE OF LIECHTENSTEIN

The inner shield represents the ancient princely family

Red and yellow are the Prince's colors

The four arms within the Prince's Arms represent his noble ancestors

Austria

Adopted Circa 1230 | **Ratio** 2:3 | **Usage** National and Civil

According to legend, the red-and-white flag was modeled after the bloodstained surcoat of a Duke wounded in battle

The traditional flag, retained after the fall of the Habsburgs in 1918

Austria once ruled much of central Europe, but lost most of its territory in 1919. Between 1938 and 1945, Austria was annexed to Germany.

Tradition states that a Duke of Austria once fought so fiercely in battle that the white surcoat he wore was soaked in blood, except for the part covered by his sword belt. So he adopted red, with a white band across the center, as his colors.

ONE OF THE WORLD'S OLDEST FLAGS

The story is probably apocryphal, but stripes of red-white-red have been an emblem of Austria for over 800 years. Their use on a flag was recorded in 1191, making the Austrian flag one of the world's oldest flags. It was officially adopted as the national flag after the fall of the Habsburg Dynasty, and the formation of a republic in 1918.

During the Second World War, the Austrian flag and arms were banned; they were restored in 1945.

ARMS OF AUSTRIA

The coat of arms depicts an imperial black eagle, an emblem used by the Habsburgs. It originally had two heads, but they were changed to one when the Habsburg Empire disintegrated. On the eagle's chest is a shield in the national colors. The eagle holds a hammer and sickle recalling agricultural and industrial workers. Its crown, with three turrets, also represents agriculture, industry, and commerce. The broken chains on the eagle's feet symbolize the restoration of freedom.

Austria: State flags

Most provincial flags in Austria are based on the local arms.
In many cases, they existed before their official adoption.

Burgenland

The colors of the flag, officially hoisted in 1971, are based on the red eagle and yellow shield of the arms.

Carinthia

Adopted in 1946, the colors are derived from those of the Austrian flag and the yellow state shield.

Lower Austria

Adopted in 1954, the colors are based on the arms which contains a blue shield and five gold eagles.

Salzburg

The flag, adopted in 1921, uses the traditional colors of the state, based on the national colors.

Styria

The coat of arms of Styria is a green shield bearing a white lion. The flag, adopted in 1960, uses these colors.

State flags (continued)

Tyrol

The bicolored flag is derived from the arms which depicts a red eagle on a white disc. It was adopted in 1945.

Upper Austria

Upper Austria's flag, adopted in 1949, is derived from the national colors and the arms of the province.

Vienna

The flag dates from 1946. It is based on the city's arms, but is identical to the flags of Salzburg and Vorarlberg.

Vorarlberg

Like the flags of Salzburg and Vienna, Vorarlberg's bicolor flag is based on the provincial arms.

Hungary

Adopted October 1, 1957 | **Ratio** 1:2 | **Usage** National and Civil

Red symbolizes strength

White represents faithfulness

Green is symbolic of hope

Part of Austria-Hungary until 1918, Hungary became part of the Communist bloc from 1945–89. In 2004, Hungary joined the European Union.

The current flag was first used in the 1848–49 uprising. Its pattern was derived from the French *Tricolore* used during the French Revolution. The colors—red, white, and green—date back to the 9th century. They were first used in 1608 during the reign of King Matthias II. Until 1945, the royal crown featured in the center of the national flag. During Hungary's brief period as a republic from 1945–49 the royal crown was replaced by the "*Kossuth*" coat of arms. When the Communists took power, they added a Soviet-style emblem to the flag. In 1990, the arms of the kingdom were readopted, but they were not replaced on the flag.

ARMS OF HUNGARY

The red and white stripes probably originated from Spain in the late 12th or early 13th century

The crown of St. Stephen, the first king of Hungary

The patriarchal cross was added to the Hungarian arms about 800 years ago

Czech Republic

Adopted March 30, 1920 | **Ratio** 2:3 | **Usage** National and Civil

The blue triangle was added to distinguish the flag from that of Poland

White and red are the heraldic colors of Bohemia (any similarity to the Pan-Slavic colors is coincidental)

Blue represents the state of Moravia

The Czech Republic was part of Austria until 1919, when it merged with Slovakia to form Czechoslovakia. The states separated in 1993.

The first flag of Czechoslovakia was based on the arms, and was white over red. This was identical to the flag of Poland, so a blue triangle was added at the hoist. The flag was banned by the Nazis in 1938, and a horizontal tricolor of white, red, and blue was enforced. The original flag was restored in 1949.

THE NEW CZECH REPUBLIC

When the Czech Republic and Slovakia separated in 1993, the Czechs decided to keep their existing flag, recalling the two principal parts of the country.

The greater coat of arms depicts a quartered shield reflecting the regions of the Czech Republic.

GREATER ARMS OF THE CZECH REPUBLIC

The white lion on a red field is the traditional emblem of Bohemia

The red-and-white eagle on a blue field is from the arms of Moravia

The black eagle on a yellow field is taken from the arms of Silesia

The Bohemian arms are repeated to fill the shield

Slovakia

Adopted September 3, 1992 | **Ratio** 2:3 | **Usage** National and Civil

A version of this flag was first used in the 19th century

White, blue, and red are Pan-Slavic colors

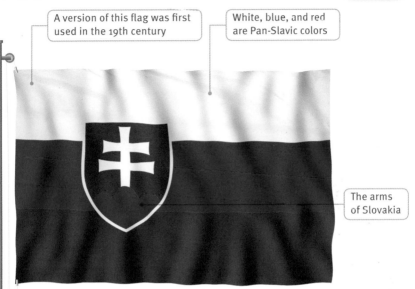

The arms of Slovakia

Under Hungarian rule until 1919, Slovakia then formed part of Czechoslovakia with the Czech Republic. The two states separated in 1993.

The first Slovak flags, used during the 19th century, were like the contemporary Russian flag, to whom they looked for aid in gaining independence. As Czechoslovakia, a red and white flag with a blue triangle was used. During the Second World War, Slovakia readopted the white, blue, and red tricolor, with the arms in the center.

ARMS OF SLOVAKIA

The arms uses colors of the early flags, a white patriarchal cross rising from blue mountains on a red shield.

On gaining independence in 1993, the red, white, and blue tricolor was retained as the national flag, but the arms was placed toward the hoist.

The President's flag has the arms, bordered by the national colors.

THE PRESIDENT'S FLAG

The flag is bordered by stripes in the national colors—white, blue, and red

A patriarchal cross

A stylized image of Slovakia's mountains

Slovenia

Adopted June 25, 1991 | **Ratio** 1:2 | **Usage** National and Civil

The order of the tricolor is the same as the flag for Slovenia, when it was part of Yugoslavia

The coat of arms was added in 1991 when Slovenia became independent

Historically under Austrian rule, Slovenia formed part of Yugoslavia in 1919. It declared independence on June 26, 1991 and joined EU in 2004.

Like Slovakia, Slovenia looked to Russia in the 19th century for assistance in gaining independence. For the same reason, the Pan-Slavic tricolor of blue, white, and red was adopted for Yugoslavia, with a gold fimbriated red star added by Tito in 1946. Slovenia also had its own flag within Yugoslavia, distinguished by the order of the stripes (white, blue, red). After independence, Slovenia placed its arms in the upper hoist of this tricolor, to create a distinct national flag.

The arms depicts mountain peaks, above wavy blue lines symbolizing the sea coast. The stars are from the arms of the Duchy of Selje.

ARMS OF SLOVENIA

The three stars are from the arms of the former Duchy of Selje

The wavy lines symbolize Slovenia's sea coast

The three mountain peaks represent the Triglav, part of the Alps

Croatia

Adopted December 21, 1991 | **Ratio** 1:2 | **Usage** National and Civil

Red, white, and blue are traditional Croatian colors

Arms of Croatia

The tricolor charged with the coat of arms was first used during the Second World War

For much of its existence, Croatia was under Austrian rule. It joined Yugoslavia in 1919, but declared independence on June 25, 1991.

While part of Yugoslavia, Croatia's flag was designed in the Pan-Slavic colors, red, white, and blue. These are also traditional Croatian colors used in the 19th century.

During the Second World War, Croatia became a semi-independent state and added the arms of Croatia to the center of its flag. Following the war,

Croatia retained its tricolor, but a gold-edged red star was placed in the center by Tito. Before gaining independence, the present flag was adopted, based on the one used during the war.

The shield of Croatia is in the red and white checks of Croatia. Above is a row of shields of its various territories.

ARMS OF CROATIA

The red and white checks are traditional emblems of Croatia

The small shields at the top are taken from the arms of Croatia's regions: the ancient arms of Croatia, Dubrovnik, Dalmatia, Istria, and Slavonia (from left to right)

Bosnia & Herzegovina

Adopted February 4, 1998 | **Ratio** 1:2 | **Usage** National and Civil

The dark blue and yellow, and the stars, refer to the flag of Europe

The flag was imposed by the international High Representative

The geographical shape of Bosnia is a triangle

Bosnia-Herzegovina was under Turkish rule until it was ceded to Austria in 1878. From 1945 to 1992, it formed part of Yugoslavia.

After Bosnia-Herzegovina broke away from Yugoslavia in 1992, a neutral plain white flag was adopted by Parliament. The country's independence triggered a civil war between the country's three ethnic groups—Muslims, Croats, and Serbs. After the Dayton, OH, peace agreement was signed in 1995, the "neutral" Bosnian flag became unacceptable to the Croats and Serbs.

In February 1998, the international High Representative, who safeguards the peace in Bosnia-Herzegovina, imposed a new flag. However, it was designed by a committee with members from all three ethnic groups.

The country's coat of arms was adopted in 1998, replacing the design that had been in use since 1992.

BOSNIA-CROAT FEDERATION FLAG

The shield's shape alludes to the shape of the country

Three-pointed shield recalls the country's three main ethnic groups

Montenegro

Adopted July 13, 2004 | **Ratio** 1:2 | **Usage** National and Civil

The flag is based on one used in the 1880s and 1890s

The modern coat of arms of Montenegro

Montenegro united with Serbia and other states in 1919, to form Yugoslavia. In 2006, Montenegro declared independence from Serbia.

Long an independent kingdom, Montenegro, like the other Yugoslav states, had used the Pan-Slav colors. Montenegro, like Serbia, inverted the Russian flag into a horizontal tricolor of red, blue, and white. In 1914, it was accepted that the royal monogram of King Nikola should be added to the flag.

In the communist state (1946–91), the monogram was replaced by a gold-edged red star. With the end of communist rule, the star was removed. To distinguish the flag from that of Serbia, the blue was made lighter. In 2004, the present—and completely different—flag was adopted.

NATIONAL FLAG IN 1914

POST-COMMUNIST FLAG

Serbia

Adopted November 11, 2010 | **Ratio** 2:3 | **Usage** National and Civil

Coat of arms appears
on the state flag

Citizens usually use the
flag without the arms

Serbia was a kingdom, until conquered by the Turks. It regained independence in the 19th century, uniting with other Balkan states to form Yugoslavia, but separated during 1991–2006 conflict.

Like the other southern Slav states, Serbia used the Pan-Slav colors by inverting the Russian flag. This example was followed by Montenegro. When Yugoslavia was formed, a flag was chosen of horizontal stripes of blue, white, and red. This used the colors of the states, in a different pattern from any of them. Under the communist state (1946–91), a gold-edged red star was added to the national flag and to the state flags. After 1991, the star disappeared and the flag often bore the Serbian coat of arms. This form became official after the final separation of Serbia and Montenegro in 2006.

**FLAG OF YUGOSLAVIA
(1919–2006)**

**FLAG OF SERBIA IN COMMUNIST
YUGOSLAVIA (1946–92)**

Kosovo

Adopted February 17, 2008 | **Ratio** 5:7 | **Usage** National and Civil

Blue and yellow are from the European Union Flag, while white is for peace

Six stars are for the six communities in Kosovo

Golden map of county outline on a blue field

Formerly part of Yugoslavia and then Serbia, Kosovo came under United Nations administration in 1999. Kosovo declared independence in February, 2008.

In 1459, the Ottoman Turks destroyed the first Serbian kingdom in a battle in modern Kosovo. Although the country was ceded to Serbia in 1913, the majority of Kosovars are Albanian in language and culture. The site of the battle, however, is sacred to the Serbs.

When Yugoslavia broke apart in the 1990s, many Kosovars hoped that they would unite with Albania. Serbia opposed this idea. In 1999, violence flared between Kosovars and Serbs. NATO forces intervened to stop Serbian attacks. In the uneasy peace that followed, there were negotiations under the United Nations. These failed, and in 2008 Kosovo controversially declared its independence.

ARMS OF KOSOVO

The arms is a shield in the same design as the flag

Albania

Adopted April 7, 1992 | **Ratio** 5:7 | **Usage** National

The traditional heraldic Albanian flag first used in 1912 when independence was restored

Albanians call their country, *Shqipëria*, meaning "land of the eagle"

Once part of the Byzantine Empire, Albania became a kingdom in 1912. From 1944 to 1991, it was a strict Communist state.

The black eagle first appeared on the Albanian flag in the 15th century when Albania became part of the Byzantine Empire. According to legend, the Albanians are the descendants of the eagle. The red flag, with the eagle in the center, was adopted in 1912, when independence was restored. Parts of the Italian arms were included on the flag after the invasion of 1939, but the original flag was restored in 1942.

In 1946, the flag changed again, to incorporate a gold-edged red star above the eagle, representing the Communist regime. The star was removed in 1991, by order of the new multiparty government.

ARMS OF ALBANIA

The black eagle has been an emblem of Albania since the 15th century

The two-headed eagle first appeared on flags used during the struggle against Turkish occupation

Macedonia

Adopted October 5, 1992 | **Ratio** 1:2 | **Usage** National and Civil

Red was the traditional color of the Macedonian flag

The radiant sun was added in 1995 to replace the controversial "Star of Vergina"

Macedonia was under Turkish rule for centuries. It united with Serbia in 1913 and became part of Yugoslavia. It declared independence in 1992.

As part of Yugoslavia, Macedonia was the only region not to use the Pan-Slavic colors. Its flag was red, with a gold-edged red star in the canton.

A CONTROVERSIAL NEW FLAG

At independence in 1992, Macedonia retained the red flag but added a gold star in a gold sun. This was soon changed to the Star of Vergina, an ancient Macedonian emblem from the tomb of Philip of Macedon, father of Alexander the Great. Greece objected to this, claiming the star as a Greek emblem. In 1995, the star was replaced by a radiant sun.

Macedonia's arms is similar in design to former Soviet emblems.

ARMS OF MACEDONIA

The star of socialism

Symmetrical wreaths of wheat

A radiant sun, also used on the national flag

Bulgaria

Adopted November 22, 1990 | **Ratio** 3:5 | **Usage** National and Civil

White and red were taken from the Pan-Slavic colors

Before 1990, the white stripe contained the Bulgarian coat of arms

The green stripe replaced the blue of the Russian tricolor

Red is for the valor of the Bulgarian army

Bulgaria became independent in 1908 after 500 years of Ottoman rule. In 1990, the Communist regime, in power since 1946, collapsed.

While under Turkish rule, Bulgaria had no national flag. When it became a principality in 1878, a slight variation of the Pan-Slavic colors, widely used during the independence movements of the late 19th century, was adopted. The horizontal arrangement of the tricolor was based on the Russian flag at the time, but for Bulgaria's national flag, the central blue stripe was substituted by green.

THE PEOPLE'S REPUBLIC

No change was made to the flag during Bulgaria's period as an independent kingdom 1908–46, but with the formation of the People's Republic in 1947, a coat of arms was added in the white stripe near the hoist. This depicted a rampant lion, a red star representing Communism, and later a cogwheel symbolizing industrialization. The coat of arms was removed from the flag in 1990 because of its Communist connotations. No arms now appear on the flag.

THE SYMBOLISM OF THE COLORS

Although based on the Pan-Slavic colors, the white band is said to represent a love of peace, and red, the valor of the people. The green stripe, substituted for the traditional Pan-Slavic blue in 1878, was intended to represent the youthfulness of the emerging nation.

Greece

Adopted January 13, 1822 | **Ratio** 2:3 | **Usage** National and Civil

The nine stripes represent the nine syllables in the cry "Freedom or Death," uttered during the Greek war of independence

White reflects the purity of the Greek independence struggle

Blue represents the sea and sky

The cross in the canton represents Greek religious faith

Once part of the Ottoman Empire, Greece has seen periodic unrest since the Second World War. In 1974 it became a multiparty democracy.

The flag flown by Greece is in the same colors as the one that was raised following independence from the Ottoman Empire in the early 19th century. At times, Greece has used a plain white cross on blue as its land flag, and the striped flag at sea. Today the plain Cross Flag is preserved in the president's flag and in the canton of the blue-and-white striped national flag.

The shade of blue of the flag has also varied. Today it is the original light blue color of 1822. It was altered in the 1970s and the blue was changed to a much darker, navy shade.

THE PRESIDENT'S FLAG

The original white cross on a blue field is retained in the president's flag and the national arms

A wreath of laurels surrounds the Cross flag

Romania

Adopted December 27, 1989 | **Ratio** 2:3 | **Usage** National and Civil

Blue formed part of the province of Moldavia's flag

Yellow formed part of the province of Wallachia's flag

Red was featured in the flags of both Moldavia and Wallachia and is the color of Romanian unity

Romania emerged from the Ottoman Empire as an independent kingdom in 1859. It is now a democracy, after decades of Communist rule.

The current flag was created in 1848 by combining the colors of Wallachia and Moldavia—the Ottoman provinces that made up Romania. In 1867, the Royal Arms was set in the yellow stripe. The coat of arms was modified many times, and in 1948, it was replaced with a Communist emblem. This was jettisoned following the fall of the Ceausescu regime in 1989.

NEW NATIONAL ARMS
In 1992, the old coat of arms was restored by the new parliament. It features a combination of motifs that look back to Romania's past as a powerful medieval state.

ARMS OF ROMANIA

The eagle grips an Eastern Orthodox cross in its beak

Sword recalls St. Stephen the Great of Moldavia

The scepter of St. Michael the Brave of Wallachia

The smaller shield displays the arms of some of Romania's provinces

Moldova

Adopted April 27, 1990 | **Ratio** 1:2 | **Usage** National and Civil

The blue, yellow, and red colors reflect strong links with Romania

The arms of Moldova

Moldova was once part of Romania, but was incorporated into the Soviet Union in 1940. It has been fully independent since 1991.

The blue, red, and yellow tricolor of Moldova is almost identical to the Romanian flag, reflecting the two countries' cultural affinity.

ARMS OF MOLDOVA

On Moldova's flag the yellow stripe is charged with the national arms. Like the Romanian coat of arms, the Moldovan arms, adopted in 1990, features a golden eagle holding an Eastern Orthodox cross in its beak. However, instead of a sword, the eagle is holding an olive branch. The blue and red shield on the eagle's breast is also different—on it are an ox's head, a star, a rose, and a crescent—all traditional symbols of Moldova.

THE ARMS OF MOLDOVA

A star

A rose

An olive branch symbolizing peace

An eagle holds an Eastern Orthodox cross, similar to that in the arms of Romania

A crescent

An ox's head

Belarus

Adopted June 7, 1995 | **Ratio** 1:2 | **Usage** National and Civil

A national ornament representing woven cloth

Red and green were the colors of Belarus's flag while it was a Soviet republic

Red and white are traditional Belarussian colors

Belarus, formerly White Russia, became independent of the USSR in 1991, although its ties with Russia are increasing once more.

The original flag of Belarus while under Soviet administration in 1922 was similar to that of the USSR. It was changed in 1951, and the flag used today is similar to this second flag, except that the Communist hammer, sickle, and star have been removed, and the red and white portions of the hoist ornamentation have been reversed.

were derived from the arms of the republic. The design was rejected in a referendum in 1995.

The flag of Belarus adopted following the referendum, reflects its growing ties with Russia. The unusual ornamentation in the hoist is described as a national ornament and represents woven cloth.

THE REJECTED DESIGN

Following independence from the USSR in 1991, Belarus adopted a flag of three equal horizontal stripes of white-red-white. This was the same flag that had been associated with a brief period of Belarussian independence in 1918, and its colors

ARMS OF BELARUS

The Soviet-style coat of arms, retained on gaining independence, also reflects the dominant Russian influence. This depicts an outline of the state against a sun rising from behind a globe. This is entirely surrounded by wreaths of wheat and flowers.

Ukraine

Adopted January 28, 1992 | **Ratio** 2:3 | **Usage** National and Civil

Originally the flag of the republic in 1918

Blue represents the sky

Yellow recalls the vast grain fields

Ukraine formed an independent state in 1918, but came under Soviet control one year later and remained so until independence in 1991.

The bicolored flag flown in Ukraine today was the official flag of the country in 1918 when Ukraine enjoyed a brief period of independence. With the invasion of the Red Army, the flag was suppressed until the German occupation of 1941–44. After the war it was banned again by the Soviet Union. When Ukraine gained its independence in 1991, the country readopted its original flag. Blue is supposed to represent the sky and yellow the vast fields of grain of the country's agriculture.

The Ukrainian coat of arms is in the national colors and features an ancient trident symbol.

ARMS OF UKRAINE

Blue and yellow are national colors

The trident is an ancient symbol dating back to pre-Roman times

The trident of St. Volodimir

Russian Federation

Adopted December 11, 1993 | **Ratio** 2:3 | **Usage** National and Civil

The colors of the flag were orginally the colors of Moscow; white, blue, and red are Pan-Slavic colors

Since its official adoption in 1799, the Russian tricolor has had a major influence on other east European flags

Russia was formed in the 15th century. The Union of Soviet Socialist Republics (USSR) was established in 1922 and included much of Asia. The USSR collapsed in 1991 and produced the Russian Federation.

At the end of the 17th century, Czar Peter the Great of Russia visited western Europe. Following this visit, he decided to adopt a variation of the Dutch flag as a civil ensign for Russian ships. This was a horizontal tricolor of white, blue, and red. It was only officially recognized in 1799. Peter the Great also adopted a flag for the Russian navy, which was white with the blue diagonal Cross of St. Andrew.

THE PAN-SLAVIC COLORS

Both the color and tricolor design of this first flag had a major influence on many of the flags of eastern European nations during the 19th century, who looked to Russia for help in liberating them from foreign domination. They have since become known as the Pan-Slavic colors.

THE HAMMER, SICKLE, AND STAR

After the Russian Revolution of 1917, the Communists abolished all former flags and instead adopted the Red Flag as the flag of the Soviet Union. This contained a gold hammer and sickle—symbols of the proletariat and the peasants—under a gold-edged red star, to represent unity. As a Soviet republic, Russia used this flag with a vertical blue bar at the hoist. When the Soviet Union collapsed in 1991, the former flags of Russia, including the white, blue, and red tricolor were restored.

Republic flags

Unlike many other countries, the flags of the Russian republics are all new, adopted since 1991.

Adygeya

Designed by a British traveler who helped resist annexation of the republic by Russia, the arrows are for resistance. Green is for agriculture and gold is for freedom.

Altay

Blue represents the clear sky, mountains, rivers, and lakes of Altay. White is for eternity, and to encourage the revival of love and harmony between the Altay people.

Bashkortostan

Blue is for charity and virtue, white for openness and willingness, and green for freedom and eternal life. The *kurai* flower represents the seven races of the Bashkir people.

Buryatia

Blue is for the sky and water, white for purity, and yellow for freedom and prosperity. The *Soembo*—the moon, sun, and hearth—recall reconciliation, family life, and hospitality.

Chechnya

Green is for Islam. Red is for the blood shed for freedom. White is the road leading to the future and the gold is the national ornament.

Republic flags (continued)

Chuvashia

The red base is the Chuvash land, from which grows the "Tree of Life." The three suns are an ancient Chuvash emblem. Gold is for future and prosperity.

Daghestan

The upper green stripe is for agriculture and hope. The blue stripe is for the Caspian Sea which borders the republic. Red represents fidelity and courage.

Ingushetia

The white stripe is for the pure intentions and actions of the people and green is for nature, fertility, and Islam. The "sun" represents peace and creativity, and its color recalls the people's struggles.

Kabardino-Balkaria

The flag's colors evoke the blue sky, the white snow-capped mountains, and the green prairies of Kabardino-Balkaria. In the center is a stylized representation of the Elbrus Mountains.

Kalmykia

The vibrant yellow is symbolic of the faith of the people of Kalmykia and also represents the sun warming their land. The blue circle signifies the eternal road to the sacred lotus in the center.

Karachay-Cherkessia

Blue symbolizes peace, kind motives, and tranquility. Green represents nature, fertility, and wealth. Red is for the warmth and unity of the people. The mountains in the center recall the scenery of the republic.

Karelia

The many lakes of Karelia are recalled by the central blue stripe and its vast pine forests by green. The red stripe symbolizes warmth, unity, and continuing cooperation between the people of Karelia.

Khakassia

The horizontal white, blue, and red stripes are taken from the Russian national flag. The vertical green stripe is for eternal life and is charged with an ancient Khakassian solar symbol.

Republic flags (continued)

Komi

The three colors of the flag recall the republic's northerly location in blue, its forests in green, and its snows in white. They are also symbolic of virtues such as cleanliness, unity, and purity.

Mari El

Mari El's flag was changed in 2011. The new emblem of the flag of Mari El is a bear. The animal, popularly known as "forest man" symbolizes the Mari people. The sword is facing down, which represents their peaceful nature.

Mordovia

The flag of Mordovia was adopted in 1995, and has the same colors as the Russian flag. In the center is the sun emblem also found on the flags of Mari El and Udmurtia.

North Ossetia

White symbolizes spirituality and cleanliness of intentions. Yellow represents the region's farming. The red stripe recalls both the Aryan people and their militant spirit in pursuit of freedom.

Tatarstan

The upper green stripe of the flag represents the majority of Muslim Tatar population of Tatarstan. The lower red stripe is for the Russian minority. The white fimbriation represents the peace that unites them.

Tuva

The original Tuvan flag adopted in 1918 was also blue, yellow, and white. Today, the colors are said to represent courage and strength in blue, prosperity in yellow, and purity in white.

Udmurtia

The eight-pointed solar sign in the center of the flag is said to guard the people from misfortune. The earth and stability are symbolized in black, morality and the cosmos in white, and life and the sun in red.

Yakutia (Sakha)

The flag recalls the blue sky and shining sun. Beneath is a white stripe recalling the snow. Red is for courage and constancy, green is for the forests of Yakutia.

Asia

Azerbaijan

Adopted February 5, 1991 | **Ratio** 1:2 | **Usage** National and Civil

The colors represent the Azerbaijani motto to "Turkify, Islamisize, and Europeanize"

Blue is often associated with the Turkic people

Green is the traditional color of Islam

Each point of the star represents a Turkic peoples

Red recalls European influence

Azerbaijan has been under consecutive Persian, Ottoman, and Russian influence. It was part of the USSR from 1920 until independence in 1991.

The flag dates back to the brief period of Azerbaijani independence during 1918–20 and replaced the one used in the Soviet era. The white crescent and eight-pointed star were intentionally similar to the emblem on the Turkish flag, since Turkey has traditionally been an ally of the country. The eight points on the flag's star stand for the eight groups of Turkic-speaking peoples—the Azeris, Ottomans, Jagatais, Tatars, Kipchaks, Seljuks, and Turkomans.

THE NATIONAL ARMS
The coat of arms, adopted in 1993, is set on a round shield in the colors of the flag.

ARMS OF AZERBAIJAN

The flame at the star's center symbolizes a new era

The shield is in the color of the national flag— blue, red, and green

The star has eight points, each representing one of the eight Turkic peoples

The golden ear of corn reflects Azerbaijan's agriculture

Armenia

Adopted August 24, 1990 | **Ratio** 1:2 | **Usage** National and Civil

Red recalls Armenian blood spilled during the struggle for independence

Blue is for hope and the Armenian skies

Orange represents the blessings of hard work

Armenia became a Soviet republic in 1922. In 1991, it gained independence from the USSR, and in 1995, held its first parliamentary elections.

Armenia achieved independence in 1918, and the flag used today comes from this era. Its origin is in a design from the Armenian Institute in Venice of 1885, although this flag used the colors red-green-blue. After independence from Russia in 1991, the Soviet flag was replaced by the 1920 tricolor of red-blue-orange.

ARMS OF ARMENIA
In 1991, the arms of 1920 replaced the Soviet coat of arms. The four emblems within the shield each represent an Armenian royal dynasty. In the center is a stylized image of Mount Ararat. The shield is supported by an eagle and a lion, common symbols in Armenian heraldry.

ARMS OF ARMENIA

Mount Ararat, the supposed resting place of Noah's Ark, is in the center of the arms

Four quarters of the shield represent former Armenian royal dynasties

Below the shield lie a broken leaf, a sheaf of wheat, a pen, and a sword

Turkey

Adopted June 5, 1936 | **Ratio** 2:3 | **Usage** National and Civil

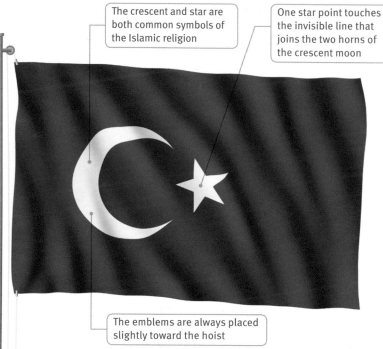

The crescent and star are both common symbols of the Islamic religion

One star point touches the invisible line that joins the two horns of the crescent moon

The emblems are always placed slightly toward the hoist

Following Turkey's defeat in the First World War, Mustafa Kemal Atatürk deposed the Sultan in 1922, and declared the country a republic in 1923.

Turkey's flag dates from 1844, although similar red flags were used as early as the 17th century within the Ottoman Empire. Between 1920–23, when Turkey became a republic, all the emblems of the Sultan were abolished and the flag became the main emblem.

THE CRESCENT AND STAR

Using the crescent and star emblems together is a relatively recent device, but the crescent on its own dates back to the Middle Ages. It is a symbol associated with Islam and also with Osman, the founder of the Ottoman Empire. The star first appeared on the flag in 1793.

Initially it had eight points, but by the early 19th century it usually had the five seen today. In 1936, the national flag and all the other flags used in Turkey today were fully defined and specified.

A PAN-ISLAMIC SYMBOL

The crescent-and-star has become an emblem of the Pan-Islamic movement sponsored by Turkey in the late 19th century; these symbols are now widely used on the flags and national arms of Muslim countries.

Turkey does not have a coat of arms, but there are individual flags for the president and senior members of the Turkish navy. These also contain the traditional crescent and star.

Georgia

Adopted January 25, 2004 | **Ratio** 3:5 | **Usage** National and Civil

Red cross, typical of St. George, Georgia's patron saint

Smaller crosses, possibly based on the "Jerusalem" cross

Georgia was absorbed into the Russian Empire in 1801 and became part of the Soviet Union in 1921. It regained independence in 1991.

During the "Rose Revolution" of 2003, the Georgian flag achieved prominence as the symbol of the opposition National Movement. On taking power in 2004, the party adopted it as the new national flag.

OBSCURE ORIGINS

The historical background of the flag is uncertain. References are made in a 14th-century text to a similar flag from Sivas, in modern Turkey. Georgians may have adopted it after invading the territory.

Another theory suggests Georgian links with the Holy Land saw the addition of the four small crosses. These were based on the "Jerusalem cross." However, it is

true that St. George is the patron saint of Georgia, perhaps explaining the basic red crosses on a white field.

THE SOVIET ERA

While part of the USSR, Georgia flew a variant of the Red Flag, adopted in 1951. It had a red field, with a thin blue stripe close to the top. The canton contained the traditional hammer, sickle, and star emblems—unusually in red and on a blue disc from which emanated 24 rays.

Following independence from the USSR in 1991, Georgia officially readopted a flag used during its brief independence between 1918 and 1921. The field was deep red, with black and white stripes in the canton.

Lebanon

Adopted December 7, 1943 | **Ratio** 2:3 | **Usage** National

The two red stripes are a symbol of self-sacrifice

The cedar tree represents holiness, eternity, and strength

The white band symbolizes peace

Lebanon became independent in 1944, after 20 years as a French mandate. The country is still recovering from many years of civil war.

The present Lebanese flag was adopted in 1943 just prior to independence from France. It was designed to be a neutral flag, not allied to any one of Lebanon's religious groups. Red is thought to be for the color of the uniforms worn by the Lebanese Legion during the First World War. Officially, the red is said to represent the people of Lebanon's sacrifice during the struggle for independence, while white represents purity.

THE CEDAR OF LEBANON

Although the flag has only existed for a little over half a century, the tree at the center of the flag—the Cedar of Lebanon—has been an emblem of the country since the time of King Solomon, almost 3,000 years ago. Specifically, the cedar is the symbol of the country's Maronite Christian community. It first appeared on a flag in 1861 when the Lebanon was part of the Ottoman Empire. Soon after its collapse, the country became mandated to France and its flag was a French *Tricolore*, with the Cedar of Lebanon in the white band of the *Tricolore*. The cedar symbolizes happiness and prosperity for the country.

The present flag, with the cedar's foliage and trunk in green, has a variant in which the tree trunk is brown—although this is not officially recognized.

Syria

Adopted March 29, 1980 | **Ratio** 2:3 | **Usage** National and Civil

An earlier version of the flag had three stars, in anticipation of a union incorporating Syria, Egypt, and Iraq

White, black, red, and green are Pan-Arab colors

The two green stars originally represented Syria and Egypt, although they are now said to represent Syria and Iraq

Syria was created after the dissolution of French colonial rule in 1946. From 1958–61 it merged with Egypt to form the United Arab Republic.

In 1920, while still a French colony, Syria flew a green-white-green tribar with a French *Tricolore* in the canton. At independence this was changed to a green, white, and black tricolor, with three red stars for its provinces across its center. Its current red-white-black Pan-Arabic flag, was adopted when Syria became part of the

United Arab Republic, but with three stars. On leaving the union in 1961, Syria briefly reverted to its original flag, before readopting the Arab Liberation colors in 1963.

The arms of Syria depicts the Hawk of Quraish, bearing a shield charged with the national flag.

ARMS OF SYRIA

The shield is in the form of a national flag

The inscription reads— in Arabic—"Arab Republic of Syria"

The hawk was the emblem of the Quraish tribe to which the Prophet Muhammad belonged

Cyprus

Adopted August 16, 1960 | **Ratio** 2:3 | **Usage** National and Civil

Neutral and peaceful symbols were chosen to represent the country

The copper-colored island recalls the origins of the country's name

The two olive branches signify peace between the Turks and Greeks

In 1960, Cyprus gained independence after almost 100 years of British rule. In 1974, the island was partitioned, following an invasion by Turkey.

Founded in 1193, the Kingdom of Cyprus experienced centuries of conflict. Cyprus was conquered by the Ottoman Empire in 1571, which increased Turkish settlement on the island. It then fell under British control in 1878. The flag, adopted at independence in 1960, deliberately chose peaceful and neutral symbols in an attempt to indicate harmony between the rival Greek and Turkish communities, an ideal that has not been realized.

In 1974, Turkish forces occupied the northern part of the island, forming the "Turkish Republic of Northern Cyprus." The two parts of the island also fly the national flags of Greece and Turkey.

THE ISLE OF COPPER

The map of the island on the flag is copper-colored, to express the meaning of the island's name—the Isle of Copper. The two olive branches on the white field represent peace between the two ethnic groups.

THE NATIONAL EMBLEM

Cyprus's national emblem is a dove holding an olive branch in its beak. This is a symbol of peace and reconciliation arising from the biblical story of Noah and the Ark. The dove is also symbolic of Aphrodite, the Greek goddess whose legend originated from the island.

Israel

Adopted October 28, 1948 | **Ratio** 8:11 | **Usage** National

The blue and white colors of the flag are derived from the Jewish prayer shawl

The central emblem is the Shield of David, which has a long association with the Jewish people

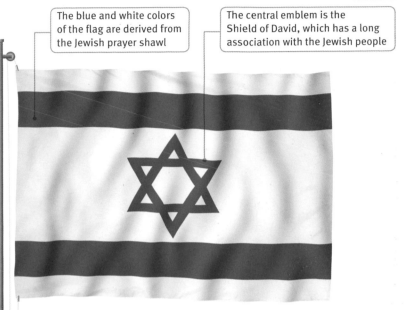

Israel gained independence in 1948. Until 1979 there were no set borders, only cease-fire lines. The situation of the Palestine people remains unsettled.

The flag was designed for the Zionist movement by David Wolfsohn in 1891, over 50 years before the state of Israel was officially declared.

STAR OF DAVID
The central emblem in the form of a hexagram is known as the "*Magen David*" (Shield of David), an emblem that had been used on Jewish flags for centuries before being adopted as the national flag of Israel. The blue and white colors are said to recall the colors of the *tallith* (Jewish prayer shawl). The blue is officially described as "Yale Blue." It is a lighter shade than is used in other Israeli flags.

The merchant flag was adopted in 1948. There is also a naval ensign of similar design.

THE CIVIL AND THE NAVAL ENSIGNS

Like other variant Israeli flags, civil (below, left) and naval (below, right) ensigns are a darker shade of blue than the national flag.

The Shield of David is slightly elongated

Jordan

Adopted April 18, 1928 | **Ratio** 1:2 | **Usage** National and Civil

Red, black, green, and white are Pan-Arab colors

The seven-pointed star represents the seven verses of Islamic belief which open the Qur'an

Originally called Transjordan, as part of the Ottoman Empire, Jordan was officially renamed when independence was gained in 1946.

The colors of the Jordanian flag are those of the Pan-Arab flag. They were first used in 1917 to represent "Pan-Arabianism," which sought independence from the Ottoman Empire. The star at the hoist was added in 1928, when Jordan gained nominal independence. It represents seven verses of Islamic belief.

JORDAN'S COAT OF ARMS
The coat of arms is similar to that designed in 1949 for the King. The crest is a crown in his honor. The current inscription on the scroll reads "The King of the Hashemite Kingdom of Jordan, Abdullah bin al-Hussein bin A'oun, Beseeches the Almighty for Aid and Success."

ARMS OF JORDAN

The current coat of arms is very similar to that designed for King Abdullah I in 1949

An Arabic inscription asking for the Almighty's aid

The crown of His Majesty the King

The black eagle symbolizes the banner of the Messenger of God

Saudi Arabia

Adopted March 15, 1973 | **Ratio** 2:3 | **Usage** National and Civil

A number of versions of the green flag have been used by the Wahabi sect since the 19th century

Green was thought to be a favorite color of the Prophet Muhammad

The *shahada*, is the Muslim Statement of Faith

The Kingdom of Saudi Arabia was unified under King Abd-al Aziz (ibn Sa'ud) in 1932. The Sa'ud family are the country's absolutist rulers.

The flag of Saudi Arabia symbolizes the Arab people of the desert. Used in various forms since the late 19th century, the green is favored by the Wahabi sect and is believed to be the favorite color of the prophet Muhammad.

FLAG INSCRIPTION

In 1901, the *shahada*, the Muslim Statement of Faith, was added to the flag in white letters, making it one of the few national flags to contain an inscription.

By law it must be able to be read correctly—from right to left—on both sides of the flag. The sword is the symbolic sword of Abd-al-Aziz, who conquered part of Arabia in the early 20th century. It has appeared in different forms in the past, sometimes as two crossed swords.

THE SHADA

The inscription reads "There is no god but Allah and Muhammad is the Prophet of Allah"

This version of the sword was added in 1981

The sword represents that given to Abd-al-Aziz by his father

Yemen

Adopted May 22, 1990 | **Ratio** 2:3 | **Usage** National and Civil

Red, white, and black, are Pan-Arab colors

The flag adopted for the united state was based on the common tricolor of former flags of North and South Yemen

Yemen was originally two countries, the Kingdom of Yemen in the north, and the British Aden Protectorate in the south. The two united in 1990.

The first flag of the Yemen, used while the Imams were in power, was red, with a white sword placed horizontally in the center, and five white stars representing the five duties of a devout Muslim. Yemen was originally two countries, each having its own flag.

SOUTH YEMEN

Formally the British Aden Protectorate, the flag of the People's Democratic Republic of Yemen was modeled on the Egyptian Pan-Arab flag. It was a red, white, and black tricolor, and it bore a blue triangle, representing the Yemeni people in the hoist, while a red star represented the Socialist ruling party.

NORTH YEMEN

The flag of the Yemen Arab Republic, formally the Kingdom of Yemen, was also modeled on the Egyptian flag. It was a red, white, and black tricolor, but it was simply charged with a single, five-pointed green star in a central white band, representing Arab unity.

A UNIFIED FLAG

When Yemen unified, the stars and the triangle were dropped, but the common elements of their flags—the Pan-Arab red, white, and black stripes—were preserved for the united flag. The new flag's pattern suggests a compromise between the officially secular south and the Islamic north.

Oman

Adopted April 25, 1995 | **Ratio** 1:2 | **Usage** National and Civil

The emblem of the ruling dynasty

White is for the Imam of Oman and for peace

The red field is common in the flags of the Gulf states

Green represents the mountains and fertility

From the mid-19th century, Oman was a British protectorate. In 1970, it achieved independence as the Sultanate of Oman.

Until 1970, Oman used the plain red banner of the indigenous people, the Kharijite Muslims. In 1970, the Sultan introduced a complete new set of national flags. Bands of green and white were added to the fly, and the national emblem, the badge of the Abusaidi Dynasty, was placed in the canton. This depicts crossed swords surmounted by a *gambia*, a traditional curved dagger.

THE SYMBOLISM OF THE COLORS
White has been associated historically with the Imam, the religious leader of Oman and at times, the political rival to the ruling Sultan. It also symbolizes peace. Green is traditionally associated with the *Jebel al Akhdar* or "Green Mountains," which lie toward the north of the country. Red is a common color in Gulf state flags.

THE NATIONAL EMBLEM

The national emblem is said to date back to the middle of the 18th century

An ornate horse's bit links the weapons

A curved dagger is fastened over a pair of crossed swords

United Arab Emirates

Adopted December 2, 1971 | **Ratio** 1:2 | **Usage** National and Civil

Historically, the flags of the emirates were plain red

Green is for trees and fertility

Black represents the oil wealth of the emirates

White symbolizes neutrality

The United Arab Emirates is an amalgamation of seven emirates, formerly known as the Trucial States, which came together in 1971.

Following a General Treaty in 1820, the seven emirates that now form the United Arab Emirates came under British protection. Red and white flags were taken up by all except the Emirate of Fujairah, a non-signatory to the treaty, which adopted a plain red flag. With minor alterations, the flags are still retained for local use. The first flag of the federation, adopted in 1968, was also red and white, but with a green star.

THE PAN-ARAB COLORS

On independence in 1971, a flag in the Pan-Arab colors—red, green, white, and black—was adopted to express Arab unity and nationalism. The red also recalls the color of the flags of the member states.

FLAG OF DUBAI

Like the other six emirates, Dubai retains its individual red and white flag

The flag colors remain constant, but the proportions have changed in recent decades

Qatar

Adopted July 9, 1971 | **Ratio** 11:28 | **Usage** National and Civil

The maroon coloring and proportions distinguish the flag from Bahrain's flag

"Qatar maroon" derives from the action of sun on natural red dye

The nine-pointed serrated line indicates that Qatar is the ninth member of the "reconciled Emirates" following a 1916 treaty

Formerly linked to Bahrain, Qatar was in a treaty relationship with Britain from 1916 until 1971, when it gained full independence.

Qatar's flag was originally plain red, like the flag of Bahrain, to which it was once linked. The peoples of both countries are Kharijite Muslims, whose traditional banner was red. The flag evolved into its present form around the middle of the 19th century, and was officially adopted when Qatar became independent from Britain in 1971.

"QATAR MAROON"
The flag's maroon color is said to have come about from the action of the desert sun's heat on the red vegetable dyes formerly used for its flags. This color, now known as "Qatar maroon," was officially adopted in 1948. The white area derives from a British request in the 1820s that all friendly

states around the Gulf add a white band to their flags, to distinguish them from pirate flags. The serrated edge indicates that Qatar is one of the nine "reconciled Emirates" that signed a treaty with Great Britain in 1916. During its earlier usage, before Qatar's independence, the flag also bore the name of the state in white lettering and red diamonds were placed on the white band.

THE EMBLEM OF QATAR
The circular badge of Qatar uses both the colors and serrated pattern of the flag around its edge. In the center is a local sailing boat, passing an island. This is set between two crossed swords. It is inscribed with the name of the state in Arabic.

Bahrain

Adopted February 14, 2002 | **Ratio** 3:5 | **Usage** National and Civil

The serrated edge was originally a straight line

Red and white are the traditional colors of the Gulf states

Despite Iran's claims of sovereignty, Bahrain, an archipelago in the Gulf, has retained its independence gained from Great Britain in 1971.

Bahrain was under British protection from 1820 to 1971. By the terms of the General Maritime Treaty of 1820, all friendly states in the Gulf undertook to add white borders to their red flags, so that they would not be taken for pirate flags. The various states of the "Pirate Coast" then developed flags with differing white patterns on them. A plain vertical white strip was added to Bahrain's flag. In 1932, the line was made serrated. In 2002, Bahrain became a kingdom, and the number of serrations was set at five.

The national arms was adopted in 1932. It is based on the colors and design of the national flag.

ARMS OF BAHRAIN

The coat of arms dates from 1932; it was designed by Sir Charles Belgrave, the Sheik's political adviser

The shield contains the characteristic serrated division line, as on the national flag

Kuwait

Adopted September 7, 1961 | **Ratio** 1:2 | **Usage** National and Civil

Black represents the defeat of the enemy

Green stands for fertility

Red symbolizes the blood of the enemy

White symbolizes purity

The State of Kuwait traces its independence to 1710, but it was under British rule from the late 18th century until 1961.

Before 1961, the flag of Kuwait, like those of other Gulf states, was red and white. The present flag is in the Pan-Arab colors, but each color is also significant in its own right. Black symbolizes the defeat of the enemy, while red is the color of blood on the Kuwaiti swords. White symbolizes purity, and green is for the fertile land.

The idea for the flag's distinctive design—a horizontal tricolor with a black trapezium in the hoist—may have come from the flag used by Iraq until the late 1950s.

KUWAIT'S COAT OF ARMS
The arms depicts a hawk above which sails an Arab *dhow* on stylized waves.

ARMS OF KUWAIT

A hawk with outstretched wings

The inscription is the name of the state

An Arab *dhow*—a traditional sailing boat

A shield in the national colors

Iraq

Adopted January 22, 2008 | **Ratio** 2:3 | **Usage** National and Civil

Red represents courage

"God is great" (*Takbir*) written in Arabic

White symbolizes generosity

Black recalls the triumphs of Islam

Iraq has been independent since 1932. The republic was proclaimed in 1958. The ousting of Saddam Hussein in 2003 has led to continued instability.

The flags of Iraq have always included the Pan-Arab colors of red, white, black, and green. The colors represent the qualities of those who follow Islam. Red represents courage; white stands for generosity; black is for the triumphs of Islam; and green is for Islam itself.

Three green stars were added to the flag in 1963, based on the then flag of Egypt (see p.104). In 1991, the inscription was added. It was modified and the stars removed in 2008.

THE NATIONAL ARMS

Also in 1963 the golden Eagle of Saladin became the national arms. It always shows the national flag on its chest.

ISLAMIC VERSE

The Islamic verse was added to the flag in 1991 and modified in 2004 and 2008

The *takbir* reads "*Allahu Akbar*" ("God is Great")

Iran

Adopted July 29, 1980 | **Ratio** 4:7 | **Usage** National and Civil

The four crescents symbolize the growth of the Muslim faith

The sword represents strength and fortitude

Kufic script from the Qur'an

The globe shape stands for the power of the world's downtrodden people

Iran was a monarchy until 1979, when the Ayatollah Khomeini deposed the Shah. An Islamic republic was formed in 1980.

The traditional green, white, and red of the Iranian flag date back to the 18th century, although there is no agreed explanation of the colors. The colors were arranged in horizontal stripes in 1906. In 1980, a new flag was introduced with the addition of emblems expressive of the Islamic Revolution.

A REVOLUTIONARY EMBLEM
The emblem in the center of the flag is a highly stylized composite of various elements representing different facets of Islamic life: Allah, the Book, the Sword, the five principles of Islam, balance, unity, neutrality, and the universal government of the downtrodden.

THE KUFIC SCRIPT (STYLIZED VERSION)

Along the edges of the green and red stripes appears the phrase "Allahu Akbar" ("God is Great")

A stylized version of Kufic script, used for the Qur'an

The script, repeated 22 times, is the date in the Islamic calendar on which Ayatollah Khomeini returned from exile in 1979

Turkmenistan

Adopted January 24, 2001 | **Ratio** 2:3 | **Usage** National and Civil

The ornamentation represents the five traditional carpet designs

Each star represents one of the five Turkmen regions

Green is a color revered in Turkmenistan

The wreath of olive leaves is identical to that on the United Nations flag, and was added in 1997

Turkmenistan was originally one of the 15 federated states of the USSR. It broke away and became an independent republic in 1991.

The original design of the flag was adopted on February 19, 1992, following a competition, and is based on national traditions. In the official interpretation, the five stars stand for the new regions established by the constitution of 1992. The carpet design contains five medallions or *guls*, said to represent the traditional designs used by the tribes who produced the country's famous carpets. The wreath of olive leaves was added in 1997 to "immortalize the policy of neutrality" declared by Turkmenistan in 1995.

The state emblem recalls the region's important agricultural products and famous horses.

STATE EMBLEM OF TURKMENISTAN

The five *guls* from the national flag

Cotton and wheat both featured on the emblem of the former Soviet Republic of Turkmenistan

An *akheltikin* horse, famed in Turkmenistan

Cotton represents the country's most important agricultural product

Uzbekistan

Adopted November 18, 1991 | **Ratio** 1:2 | **Usage** National and Civil

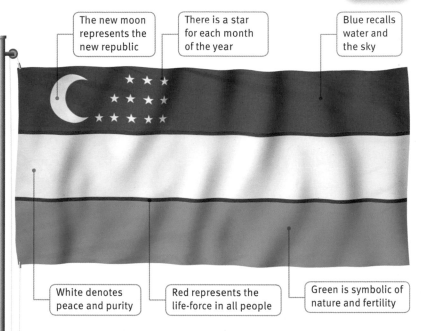

The new moon represents the new republic

There is a star for each month of the year

Blue recalls water and the sky

White denotes peace and purity

Red represents the life-force in all people

Green is symbolic of nature and fertility

Once part of the Mongol Empire, Uzbekistan fell to Russia in the late 19th century. It became independent from the USSR in 1991.

Uzbekistan was the first of the Central Asian republics to adopt its own non-Communist national flag, although the new design is based on that of the former Soviet Uzbekistan.

The blue stripe symbolizes water and the sky. It is also the color of the flag of Timur, who ruled an Uzbek empire in the 14th century. The white stripe is a sign of peace and purity. Green is a Muslim symbol of nature and fertility. Red is for the life-force found in all people. The new moon suggests the birth of the new republic, while the 12 stars represent the months of the Islamic calendar.

STATE EMBLEM OF UZBEKISTAN

The emblem features a bird whose outstretched wings form a crescent, framing a rising sun over a landscape of mountains and rivers

Cotton is Uzbekistan's chief cash crop

Islamic crescent and star

Wheat represents the country's staple food crop

The ribbon bears the name of the state

Kazakhstan

Adopted June 4, 1992 | **Ratio** 1:2 | **Usage** National and Civil

The sky blue field symbolizes the skies stretching over the many Kazakh people

A *berkut*, or steppe eagle, beneath a shining sun

The traditional "national ornamentation" is placed close to the hoist

Part of Central Asia conquered by Russia in the 18th century, Kazakhstan was the largest republic to secede from the USSR.

Kazakhstan's post-Communist flag was adopted in 1992. Its sky blue background recalls the endless skies over the Kazakh people. It also symbolizes well-being, tranquility, peace, and unity. In the center of the flag, below a golden sun with 32 rays, soars a bird of the species known locally as the *berkut*, or steppe eagle.

Together they represent love, freedom, and the aspirations of the Kazakh people. A pattern of what is described as "national ornamentation" forms a vertical stripe near the hoist.

The new state emblem is also based around a radiant sun. It depicts traditional features of Kazakhstan.

STATE EMBLEM OF KAZAKHSTAN

The center of the emblem is like the upper part of a *yurt*, the ancient felt tent of the Kazakh nomads

The sun's rays spread out like a *yurt*'s supporting structure

Winged and horned horses represent historical traditions and beliefs

Mongolia

Adopted January 12, 1992 | **Ratio** 1:2 | **Usage** Civil and State

The *soyonbo* device combines a number of Buddhist emblems

Sky blue is the national color of Mongolia

Originally the color of Communism, red today represents progress

After a decade of Communist rule, the remote state of Mongolia has been a multi-party democracy since 1996.

The current national flag replaced the Red Flag of revolution in 1940. The red field is retained at the fly and hoist, although the color's original Socialist connotations have given way to more general themes of progress and prosperity. The sky blue panel represents the people of Mongolia and invokes the imperial days of Genghis Khan. The flag bears a 17th-century Buddhist emblem at hoist called the *soyonbo*. The *soyonbo* comprises various ideograms representing different elements from the Buddhist view of the world. The Communist star that appeared above the *soyonbo* was removed in 1992.

THE *SOYONBO*

The sun and moon represent ancestors of the Moguls

Horizontal bars indicate that vigilance is required from the highest and lowest in society

The tongues of the flame stand for past, present, and future

The vertical columns illustrate the Mongolian proverb "Two friends are stronger than stone"

The fish stand for vigilance because fish never sleep

Kyrgyzstan

Adopted March 3, 1992 | **Ratio** 3:5 | **Usage** National and Civil

Red is for Manas the Noble, the national hero

The sun's 40 rays stand for the 40 tribes and 40 heroes of the Kyrgyz nation

A stylized *yurt*, the traditional home of nomadic people

Conquered by Russia under the czars, in 1991 the Republic of Kyrgyzstan became the last of the Soviet Union Republics to declare sovereignty.

Independent since 1991, a post-Communist flag was not adopted until 1992. The flag's red background is supposed to be the flag color used by the national hero, Manas the Noble, who welded 40 tribes together to form the Kyrgyz nation.

In the center of the flag is a yellow sun with 40 rays, representing the tribes and the legendary 40 heroes of Manas. The sun's rays run clockwise on the obverse of the flag and counterclockwise on the reverse.

A TRADITIONAL *YURT*

At the sun's center is a stylized bird's-eye view of the roof, or *tunduk*, of a Kyrgyz *yurt*, the traditional tent used by the nomadic people of the steppe. It symbolizes the unity of time and space, the origin of life, hearth and home, and the history of the nomads.

ARMS OF KYRGYZSTAN

Like the arms of its neighbor, Kazakhstan, the coat of arms of Kyrgyzstan is round and does not contain a traditional shield. In the center is a white eagle with spread wings. Behind this are snowcapped mountains, representing the mighty Tien Shan, and a radiant, rising sun. This scene is bordered by wreaths of cotton and wheat, both major agricultural products in Kyrgyzstan. The name of the state is inscribed in Cyrillic script at the top.

Tajikistan

Adopted November 24, 1992 | **Ratio** 1:2 | **Usage** National and Civil

The crown and stars stand for Tajikistan's state sovereignty

White is the color of cotton, Tajikistan's main industry

Green represents farm produce

A former member of the USSR, Tajikistan proclaimed independence in 1991, but Russian influences remain strong.

In 1992, Tajikistan became the last of the former USSR republics to adopt a new flag. The red, white, and green stripes are the same as those chosen in 1953 for the flag of the Tadzhik Soviet Socialist Republic. Red is the color of the flag of the USSR; white is for cotton, Tajikistan's main export; and green recalls other farm produce.

SYMBOLS OF THE NEW STATE
The center of the flag features a gold crown and an arc of seven stars. These symbols refer to the state sovereignty of Tajikistan, friendship between all nations, and the "unbreakable union of workers, peasants, and the intellectual classes" of the republic.

STATE EMBLEM OF TAJIKISTAN

The flag colors of red, white, and green

The mountains recall the country's many peaks

Crown and stars from the national flag

Wheat and cotton, both major crops, surround the arms

Afghanistan

Adopted January 4, 2004 | **Ratio** 2:3 | **Usage** National

Black recalls previous flags used in Afghanistan

The new arms of Afghanistan

Green represents Islam

Afghanistan has had a troubled history. This is reflected by no less than 14 distinct national flags it has used in the 20th and 21st centuries.

With the election of a democratic government in 2004, the present flag was adopted. Black, red, and green have been traditional in most Afghan flags. Black is from the first recognized Afghan flag, red is for bravery, and green for Islam. The white emblem in the center is the state coat of arms. This too is a traditional design.

The arms show the Muslim Mehrab (the niche that shows the direction to the Muslim Holy City of Mecca) and Minbar (the pulpit from which sermons are preached). These are shown within a traditional image of a mosque, flanked by two national flags and surrounded by sheaves of wheat. Four inscriptions also appear at the top and bottom of arms.

ARMS OF AFGHANISTAN

The Arabic inscription "God is Great"

The date 1298 in the Muslim calendar (AD 1919), is the date Afghanistan was internationally recognized as an independent state

The Arabic inscription reads: "There is no god but Allah, and Muhammad is the Prophet of Allah"

The name of Afghanistan in Arabic script

Pakistan

Adopted August 11, 1947 | **Ratio** 2:3 | **Usage** National

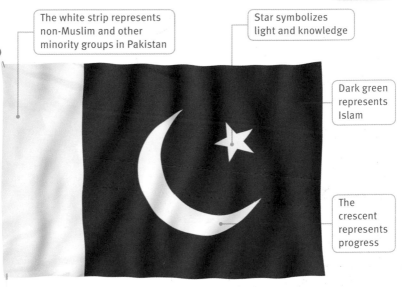

The white strip represents non-Muslim and other minority groups in Pakistan

Star symbolizes light and knowledge

Dark green represents Islam

The crescent represents progress

Once a part of British India, Pakistan was created in 1947 as an independent Muslim state. Today, it is divided into four provinces.

The flag was designed by Muhammad Ali Jinnah, founder of the nation. It is associated with the flag used by the All-India Muslim League as an emblem of its aim of achieving an independent Muslim state. Their flag was green, with a central white star and crescent. At independence, a white stripe was added at the hoist to represent the state's minorities.

THE SYMBOLISM OF THE COLORS
The green and white together stand for peace and prosperity. The crescent symbolizes progress and the star represents light and knowledge.

The flag of the president is similar to the national flag. The emblems are in gold and are enclosed within a wreath of laurel. Beneath is the name of the state in Urdu.

THE PRESIDENT'S FLAG

The field of the president's flag is green and white, like the national flag

The crescent and star are symbols of Islam

The name of the state is written in Urdu

Nepal

Adopted December 16, 1962 | **Ratio** 11:9 | **Usage** National and Civil

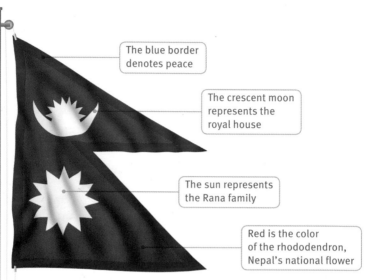

The blue border denotes peace

The crescent moon represents the royal house

The sun represents the Rana family

Red is the color of the rhododendron, Nepal's national flower

From 1960, Nepal was ruled by an absolute monarchy. This regime ended in 1991 when the first multiparty elections were held.

The flag of Nepal is the only national flag that is not rectangular or square. Originally, two separate triangular pennants were flown one above the other; these were then joined to form a single flag. Its crimson red is the color of the rhododendron—the country's national flower. Red is also the sign of victory in war. The blue border is the color of peace.

THE SUN AND THE MOON
Until 1962, the flag's emblems, the sun and the crescent moon, had human faces. They were removed to modernize the flag. The sun retains the face on the Royal Standard. The crescent represents the royal house and the sun denotes the Rana family, the hereditary prime ministers until 1961.

THE ROYAL STANDARD (1960–2008)

The Royal Standard shows a rampant lion holding a lance with a flag

The sun has a face, as did the national flag until 1962

Bhutan

Adopted Circa 1965 | **Ratio** 2:3 | **Usage** National and Civil

Saffron yellow denotes the authority of the King

The "Thunder Dragon"

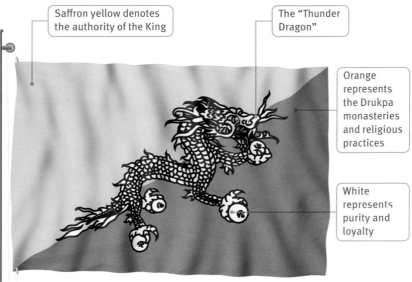

Orange represents the Drukpa monasteries and religious practices

White represents purity and loyalty

Bhutan is a Buddhist state where power is shared by the king and government. The country's name in the local dialect means "Land of the Dragon."

In Bhutan, thunder is believed to be the sound of dragons roaring. In about 1200, a monastery called the *Druk* (the "Thunder Dragon"), was set up, with a sect called the Drukpas named after it. The name and the emblem of the dragon have been associated with Bhutan ever since. The dragon on the flag is white to symbolize purity.

TEMPORAL AND SPIRITUAL POWER
The two colors of the flag, divided diagonally, represent spiritual and temporal power within Bhutan. The orange part of the flag represents the Drukpa monasteries and Buddhist religious practice, while the saffron yellow field denotes the secular authority of the royal dynasty of the Wangchuks.

EMBLEM OF BHUTAN

The dragon symbolizes *Druk*, the Tibetan name for the Kingdom of Bhutan

The snarling mouth expresses the strength of the male and female deities protecting the country

Jewels clasped in the dragon's claws symbolize wealth

India

Adopted July 22, 1947 | **Ratio** 2:3 | **Usage** National

Orange represents courage and sacrifice

The *Chakra*, or Buddhist spinning wheel

White symbolizes peace and truth

Green symbolizes faith and chivalry

Under British rule from 1763, the Indian subcontinent divided into Pakistan and India in 1947 upon independence.

The national flag, adopted in 1947, is based on the flag of the Indian National Congress, which was established in 1885 to press for independence. The flag's orange color symbolizes courage and sacrifice, white stands for peace and truth, green is for faith and chivalry, and blue represents the color of the sky and the ocean.

THE CHAKRA

The central motif is a *Chakra*, or Buddhist spinning wheel. The 24 spokes of the wheel correspond with the 24 hours of the day, implying that there is life in movement and death in stagnation. The naval ensign is adapted from British practice. The gold National Emblem was added in 2004.

INDIAN NAVAL ENSIGN

The national flag is placed in the canton

The gold National Emblem of India appears in the center

The design derives from British naval practice

Maldives

Adopted July 25, 1965 | **Ratio** 2:3 | **Usage** National and Civil

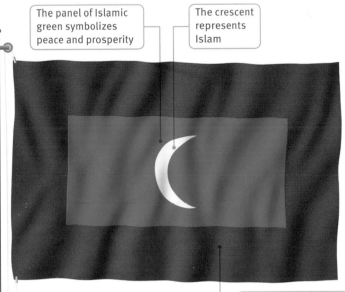

The panel of Islamic green symbolizes peace and prosperity

The crescent represents Islam

Red was the original color of the Maldives flag

The archipelago of small islands that forms the Maldives was once a British Protectorate. The Maldives became fully independent in 1965.

Until the beginning of the 20th century the flag of the Maldives was plain red, reflecting the culture of the Arab traders from the Persian Gulf who operated among the islands. This flag remained in use after the British Protectorate was set up in 1887. The flag later acquired a white crescent facing the hoist—another sign of Islamic influence.

A NEW DESIGN

The flag was redesigned in 1948 after the independence of Ceylon (now Sri Lanka), of which the islands had been a dependency. The crescent was turned around and placed on an Islamic green panel. A pattern of black and white diagonal stripes was added along the hoist. This was dropped after independence from Britain in 1965. A modern interpretation of the colors suggests that red symbolizes the blood shed in the struggle for independence, while green stands for peace and progress.

THE NATIONAL EMBLEM

The national emblem of the Maldives contains the Islamic crescent and star emblem beneath a date palm. Below the crescent is a scroll with the inscription, in Dihevi, "State of a Thousand Islands," which recalls the many islands—over 2,000—that make up the Maldives. The crescent is flanked by two national flags.

Sri Lanka

Adopted December 17, 1978 | **Ratio** 1:2 | **Usage** National and Civil

Orange represents Hindus

The four *pipul* leaves are Buddhist symbols

Green represents Muslims

The sword is a symbol of authority

The island of Ceylon was a British colony until independence in 1948. It became a republic under the name Sri Lanka in 1972.

The original flag of Sri Lanka featured just the lion and sword on a red field, recalling that the Sinhalese word for lion—"Sinhala"—is the basis of the island's name. The flag's yellow border symbolized the protection of the nation by Buddhism.

The flag was derived from the flag of the Sinhalese kingdom of Kandy. It proved unpopular with minority groups, so vertical bands of green, for Muslims, and orange, for the Hindu Tamils, were added in 1951.

When the country's name changed from Ceylon to Sri Lanka in 1972, four leaves were added. They denote the tree under which Siddhartha sat when he received enlightenment and became the Buddha. This version of the flag was in official use from 1978.

FLAG OF KANDY

The "Lion Flag" was the national flag of Ceylon prior to 1815 when it became a British colony

The finials are derived from the spire on top of a Buddhist temple

Bangladesh

Adopted January 17, 1972 | **Ratio** 3:5 | **Usage** National

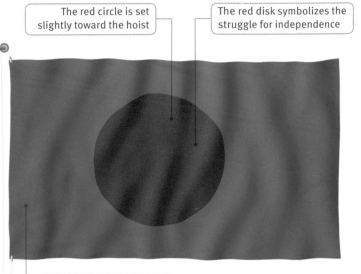

The red circle is set slightly toward the hoist

The red disk symbolizes the struggle for independence

Green represents the land

Bangladesh was formerly the eastern province of Pakistan. After a civil war with Pakistan, it became a separate country in 1971.

The flag was originally adopted in March 1971, when the country gained independence, at which time it had a yellow silhouette map of the country in the red disk. This flag was used throughout the struggle for independence, but when the state was formally established in 1971, the outline map was omitted from the new national flag.

NATIONAL EMBLEM OF BANGLADESH
The coat of arms was adopted in 1972. It consists of the national flower, a water lily, known locally as the *shapla*, growing from stylized waves. Around it are ears of rice, and above is a sprig of jute, with four golden stars. The emblem appears in the center of the president's flag, set on a deep purple field.

THE PRESIDENT'S FLAG

Wreath of rice

A *shapla* (water lily) on stylized waves

The name of the state in Bangla

A sprig of jute, with four golden stars representing nationalism, socialism, democracy, and secularism

Burma

Adopted October 21, 2010 | **Ratio** 4:7 | **Usage** National and Civil

Yellow symbolizes solidarity

Green represents peace and tranquillity

Red is for courage and decisiveness

The white star is from the flag of the Burman Resistance in the Second World War

In 1886, Burma became a province of British India. It separated from India in 1937, and gained independence from British colonial control in 1948.

Burma's flag came into use in 2010, having been introduced in the 2008 constitution. It is completely different from the two flags that Burma had had since independence. The old flags were red with a blue canton featuring six stars and later a socialist emblem. The new flag features three stripes and a single large star, similar to that on one of Burma's pre-independence flags, that of the Burman Resistance.

The emblem was also changed by the 2008 constitution. A map of Burma within a laurel wreath is surrounded by an ornate structure that incorporates two Burmese lions, a star and a scroll with the name of the country in Burmese script.

EMBLEM OF BURMA

The central emblem is guarded by two ornate Burmese lions

The central emblem is a map of Burma

Thailand

Adopted September 28, 1917 | **Ratio** 2:3 | **Usage** National and Civil

Red symbolizes lifeblood

Blue represents the monarchy

The blue and white stripes were added during the First World War

White stands for the purity of the Buddhist faith

Formerly known as the Kingdom of Siam, Thailand is the only Southeast Asian nation never to have been colonized.

Thailand is also known as the "Land of the White Elephant," and this emblem appeared on its plain red flag in the 19th century. During the First World War, horizontal white stripes were added above and below the elephant.

In 1917 the elephant was abandoned, and a blue stripe was added to the middle of the flag in order to express solidarity with the Allies, whose flags were mostly red, white, and blue. This flag is known as the *Trairanga (tricolor)*.

The Royal Arms of Thailand was introduced in 1910. The arms features the *garuda*, a bird-man in Hindu mythology.

ARMS OF THAILAND

The *garuda* of Hindu mythology is the enemy of all things poisonous

The red *garuda* is placed on a field of royal yellow for the Royal Standard

Laos

Adopted December 2, 1975 | **Ratio** 2:3 | **Usage** National and Civil

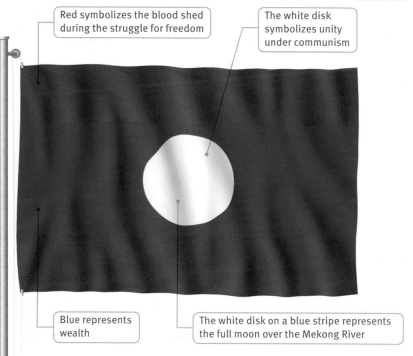

Red symbolizes the blood shed during the struggle for freedom

The white disk symbolizes unity under communism

Blue represents wealth

The white disk on a blue stripe represents the full moon over the Mekong River

A French Protectorate from the end of the 19th century, Laos gained full independence in 1953. It has been under communist rule since 1975.

The national flag of Laos was adopted in 1975, when the country became a people's republic. It is one of the few Communist flags that does not use the five-pointed star as an emblem. This flag replaced the original flag of Laos, which was red, with a triple-headed white elephant on a pedestal beneath a parasol. This expressed the ancient name of the country, "Land of a Million Elephants," and dated from the 19th century.

A FLAG FOR THE REPUBLIC

From 1953 onward, the royal government waged war with the Pathet Lao, whose flag was blue with a white disk and red borders at the top and bottom. From 1973–75, the Pathet Lao formed part of the government coalition, before assuming power directly and prompting the abdication of the king. Their flag was then adopted as the national flag.

In the center is a white disk, symbolizing the unity of the people under the leadership of the Lao People's Revolutionary Party and the country's bright future. The red stripes stand for the blood shed by the people in their struggle for freedom, and the blue symbolizes their prosperity.

The white disk on a blue background is also said to represent a full moon against the Mekong River.

Cambodia

Adopted June 29, 1993 | **Ratio** 2:3 | **Usage** National and Civil

Red and blue are traditional colors

The famous temple of Angkor Wat has appeared in various forms on Cambodia's flag

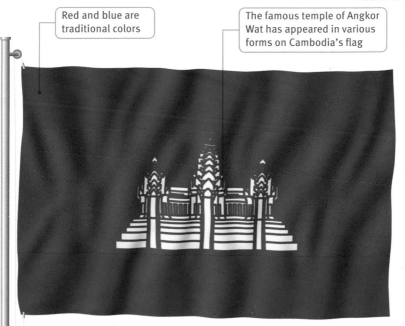

Cambodia was a French Protectorate until 1949 when it became nominally independent once more. Full independence was achieved in 1953.

The flag used today is the same as that established in 1948, although since then five other designs have been employed. These have almost all made use of the image of the temple of Angkor Wat in one form or another. This famous temple site, dating from the 12th century, was built by the Mahidharapura monarchs. It has five towers, but these were not always all depicted in the stylized version used on flags. The temple also appears on the arms. The monarchy was restored in September 1993, the 1948 flag having been readopted in June of that year.

STATE EMBLEM OF CAMBODIA

The glowing sun represents national rebirth

The inscription is the name of the country

Angkor Wat is a symbol of the nation and its greatness

Vietnam

Adopted November 30, 1955 | **Ratio** 2:3 | **Usage** National and Civil

Red symbolizes revolution and bloodshed

The gold five-pointed star is for the unity of five groups of workers in building socialism

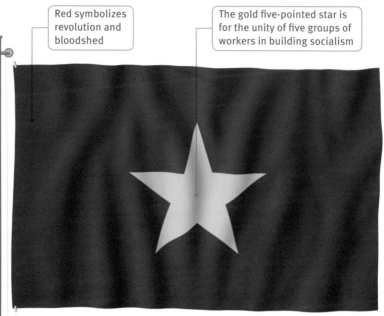

In 1954, Vietnam was divided into north and south. In 1976, the north finally achieved its aim of reunification under communism.

Vietnam's national flag was adopted in 1976, at the end of the Vietnam War, when North and South Vietnam were reunited under the new name of the Socialist Republic of Vietnam. This flag had been used by Communist North Vietnam since 1955, a year after partition.

It is essentially the same as the flag used by the national resistance movement, led by Ho Chi Minh, in its struggle against the occupying Japanese forces during the Second World War.

SYMBOLISM OF THE COLORS
The red color of the field stands for the revolution and for the blood shed by the Vietnamese people.

The five-pointed yellow star represents the unity of workers, peasants, intellectuals, youths, and soldiers in the building of socialism

NATIONAL EMBLEM OF VIETNAM
The national emblem, which was also readopted in 1976, had been used by North Vietnam since 1956. It depicts a cogwheel, symbolic of industry, and the yellow five-pointed star of socialism, enclosed by a garland of rice—the country's main agricultural product. The name of the country is inscribed on a scroll at the base of the emblem. The symbols on both the arms and the flag were inspired by the Chinese flag.

Malaysia

Adopted September 16, 1963 | **Ratio** 1:2 | **Usage** National and Civil

The crescent and star of Islam

The blue canton represents unity of the Malaysian people

The 14 red and white stripes represent the 14 states of the Federation

Malaya became independent of Britain in 1957. In 1963, the Federation of Malaysia was formed, although Singapore seceded in 1965.

The first flag of independent Malaya was based on the Stars and Stripes of the United States of America, combined with Islamic symbolism. It had 11 red and white stripes and a blue canton, like the US flag, with a gold crescent and an eleven-pointed star, traditionally associated with Islam. Both the number of stripes and points on the star denoted the 11 states of the Federation.

THREE NEW STATES

In 1963, three new states—Singapore, Sabah, and Sarawak—joined the Federation to form Malaysia. To reflect this, the flag was amended to 14 red and white stripes representing the 14 states. When Singapore seceded in 1965, the flag remained unaltered. The fourteenth stripe is now said to stand for the federal district of Kuala Lumpur.

THE SYMBOLISM OF THE COLORS

The blue canton represents the unity of the Malaysian people. The crescent is for Islam, the dominant religion. The 14 points of the star are for unity among the states of the country. Yellow is the traditional color of the rulers of the Malay states. Red and white are also traditional colors in Southeast Asia.

The national motto appears on a scroll in the coat of arms. It is repeated in both Jawi and Roman script, and means "Unity is Strength."

Malaysia: State flags

The flags of the Malaysian states were mostly derived from those of the 19th century, and were originally flags of the princes or sultans.

Johore

The blue field represents the government. The red canton is for the "*Hulubalang*" warrior caste, who defend the state. The crescent and star represent the ruler.

Kedah

Red is the traditional color of Kedah. The sheaves of yellow paddy or rice, are for prosperity. The green crescent signifies Islam, and the yellow shield is for sovereignty.

Kelentan

The red field is symbolic of the loyalty and sincerity of the people, while the white emblem represents the ruler. Kelentan has 36 royal and official flags.

Kuala Lumpur

Blue is for the unity of the population of Kuala Lumpur; red is for courage and vigor; white is for purity, cleanliness, and beauty; and yellow is for sovereignty and prosperity.

Labuan

The colors are those of the national flag and they have the same symbolism—white recalls the purity of Buddhism and red represents the lifeblood of the people.

Melaka

The colors and pattern are taken from the national flag. Unlike the Malaysian flag, the flag of Melaka has only two stripes—one in red and one in white—and a five-pointed star.

Negeri Sembilan

This flag reflects the hierarchy of power in Malaysia. The yellow field symbolizes the ruler; the black triangle, the district rulers; and the red triangle, the people.

Pahang

White is for the ruler, because it can change to any other color, reflecting how a ruler can be influenced by popular opinion. Black represents the people standing firm.

State flags (continued)

Perak

The three stripes represent different levels of the royal family. The Sultan is evoked by white, the Raja Muda by yellow, and the Raja di-Hilir by black. The latter two are junior members of the ruling family.

Perlis

Yellow represents the ruler, and blue represents the people. The colors are arranged as two equal horizontal stripes to signify the close cooperation that should exist between the ruler and his subjects.

Pinang

Light blue represents the blue seas around the island of Pinang. White is for the peace and serenity of the state, and yellow for its prosperity. The tree is the Pinang palm, after which the state is named.

Sabah

The zircon blue (top stripe) is for tranquillity, white for purity and justice, red for courage, ice blue (canton) for unity and prosperity, and royal blue for strength. The mountain is Kinabalu.

Sarawak

Yellow is the traditional color of Borneo, where the state lies. Red and black are from the flag of the former Raja of Sarawak. The star has nine points for the nine districts of the state.

Selangor

The yellow and red quarters are symbolic of flesh and blood, the combination necessary for life. The crescent and star in the canton represent Islam, the dominant religion of the state.

Terengganu

The white background stands for the Sultan. It envelopes the black field, symbolizing the people. This reflects how the Sultan provides protection to his subjects.

Indonesia

Adopted August 17, 1945 | **Ratio** 2:3 | **Usage** National and Civil

The flag is based on the banner of the 13th-century Indonesian Empire

Red represents the body

White symbolizes the soul

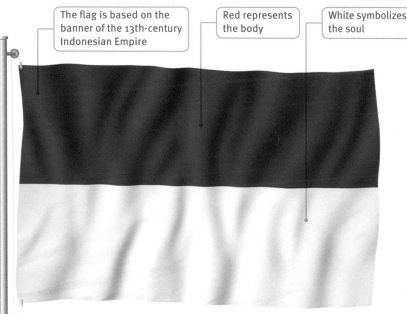

A former Dutch colony, Indonesia gained independence in 1949. Western New Guinea (Irian Jaya) was ceded to Indonesia in 1963.

The flag is based on the banner of the 13th-century Empire of Majahapit, red and white being the holy colors of Indonesia at that time. These colors were revived in the 20th century as an expression of nationalism against the Dutch. The first red and white flag flew in Java in 1928 and was adopted as the national flag of the republic in 1945 when the country declared its independence. The red stripe is symbolic of physical life, while white represents spiritual life. Together they stand for the complete human being, body and soul. Red and white are also traditional colors of the Southeast Asian nations.

NATIONAL EMBLEM OF INDONESIA

The emblem shows a shield supported by a mythical bird, the *garuda*. The 17 wing-feathers and 8 tail-feathers refer to the day and month (August 17) on which independence was declared in 1945

The shield depicts a buffalo head, a banyan tree, and sheaves of rice and cotton

The yellow star represents religious belief

The national motto means "Unity in Diversity"

East Timor

Adopted May 20, 2002 | **Ratio** 1:2 | **Usage** National and Civil

Black represents the oppression of the past

Yellow represents the wealth of the country

Red stands for the struggle for national liberation

The white star symbolizes hope

East Timor voted for independence from Indonesia in 1999. A UN administration was in place until official independence on May 20, 2002.

At midnight on May 19, 2002, the UN flag was removed from outside the government offices in Dili, the capital. The new country, now a member of the United Nations, has struggled to overcome the legacy of decades of occupation.

NEW STATE, OLD FLAG
The flag illustrated above is actually the flag designed by the Fretilin party for the "Democratic Republic of Timor" in 1975, following the transition from Portuguese colony to independence. However, the infant nation's subsequent invasion and occupation by Indonesia led to the adoption of that country's flag for the last quarter of the 20th century.

SYMBOLISM OF THE FLAG
The black triangle represents the darkness of four centuries of colonial oppression under the Portuguese. The golden-yellow arrowhead recalls the long struggle for independence, as well as the hope of the country's future prosperity. The red field reflects the blood shed by the Timorese people on their journey toward autonomy—a symbol that has taken on greater poignancy since the referendum for independence and the massacre of thousands of East Timorese by pro-Indonesian militias in 1999. The white of the star symbolizes peace, while the star itself represents the guiding light, which gives hope for the future.

Singapore

Adopted December 3, 1959 | **Ratio** 2:3 | **Usage** National and Civil

The crescent is for the new nation

The five stars symbolize ideals of democracy, peace, progress, justice, and equality

Red stands for universal brotherhood and equality

White represents the purity and virtue of the Singaporean people

Granted self-government by Britain in 1959, Singapore became part of the Federation of Malaysia in 1963, and fully independent in 1965.

The flag dates from when Singapore became a self-governing British colony in 1959. It was preserved when Singapore joined the Malaysian Federation and adopted as the national flag when Singapore became fully independent in 1965.

The colors of red and white are those of the Malay people. Red is supposed to represent universal brotherhood and equality, while white symbolizes purity and virtue. The white crescent signifies the new nation of Singapore, while the five stars next to it represent the ideals of democracy, peace, progress, justice, and equality.

The President's flag is a plain red field with the crescent and star emblem in the center.

THE PRESIDENT'S FLAG

The President's flag simply enlarges and centers the crescent and stars motif from the national flag

Red and white represent the Malay people

Brunei

Adopted September 29, 1959 | **Ratio** 1:2 | **Usage** National and Civil

Black and white stripes represent Brunei's chief ministers

The national emblem was placed in the center in 1959

Yellow represents the Sultan of Brunei

Brunei became a British Protectorate in 1888. It gained full independence in 1984, and is now an absolute monarchy under its Sultan.

A similar version of this flag, without the coat of arms, was first used in 1906. The flag's main color, yellow, is associated with the Sultan, while the black and white stripes that cut across it are the colors of the Brunei's two chief ministers. The coat of arms in the center of the flag was added in 1959.

THE NATIONAL ARMS

The coat of arms bears testament to Brunei's Muslim traditions with the crescent, a traditional symbol of Islam, at its center. The Arabic motto on the crescent translates as, "Always render service by God's guidance," below it, a scroll bears the inscription "*Brunei Darussalam*" (City of Peace).

STATE EMBLEM OF BRUNEI

The central mast is a symbol of the state

The crescent is symbolic of the Islamic faith

The flag and umbrella are symbols of royalty

The upturned hands signify the benevolence of the government

The inscription is the country's official title "*Brunei Darussalam*"

Philippines

Adopted May 19, 1898 | Ratio 1:2 | Usage National and Civil

The white triangle symbolizes purity and peace

Blue represents patriotism

Red symbolizes bravery

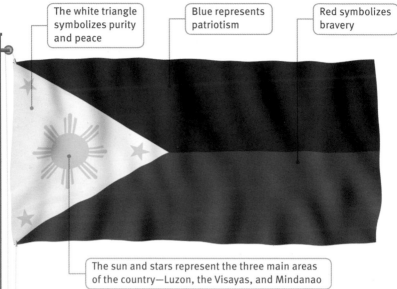

The sun and stars represent the three main areas of the country—Luzon, the Visayas, and Mindanao

The Philippines was a Spanish colony until 1898, when it was ceded to the United States of America. It gained its independence in 1946.

The flag was first used by Filipino nationalists in exile while the Spanish still controlled the islands. When they were ceded to the USA, the Philippines became far more autonomous, and the flag was flown freely from 1898. It was banned by the Americans from 1907–19, and the Stars and Stripes was flown exclusively on the islands.

The sun and stars are Masonic in origin. The eight rays of the sun are for the eight provinces that revolted against the Spanish. The three stars represent the country's three main geographical areas. White stands for purity and peace, red for bravery, and blue for patriotism. When used at war, the red stripe is flown at the top of the flag, representing courage.

THE PRESIDENT'S FLAG

The sun is taken from the national flag

The three stars and a golden sealion were adapted from the arms of Manila

A ring of 52 white stars of Manila

Taiwan

Adopted October 28, 1928 | **Ratio** 2:3 | **Usage** National

A blue flag with a white sun was the party flag of the Kuomingtang; each ray represents two hours of a day

The flag is said to represent "a white sun in a blue sky over red land"

Red recalls the Han Chinese, the dominant race in China

Taiwan was formerly part of China. It became a separate state in 1949 under the Nationalist Party, which was expelled from government in Beijing.

The flag adopted for Taiwan, or Formosa, as it was known, had been the national flag of China. It was used from 1928–49 when the Kuomingtang, the Chinese Nationalist Party, was in power.

The red field represents China, the blue canton, and white sun was the party flag of the Kuomingtang. The 12 rays of sunshine symbolize unending progress, each ray represents two hours of the day.

THE TAIPEI OLYMPIC FLAG
This flag was adopted by Taiwan in 1980 specifically for use at the Olympic Games, where its national flag was not accepted. It combines red, white, and blue—the national colors of Taiwan and the Olympic emblem.

THE TAIPEI OLYMPIC FLAG

The sun symbol is taken from the national flag

Blue, red, and white are the national colors

The emblem of connected rings shows that it is an Olympic flag

China

Adopted October 1, 1949 | **Ratio** 2:3 | **Usage** National and Civil

The large star represents communism

The red field symbolizes the Communist revolution and is also the traditional color of the Chinese

The use of five stars reflects the importance of the number five in Chinese philosophy

The four smaller stars represent the social classes of the Chinese people

China has the world's oldest continuous civilization. The Communist Chinese People's Republic was established following the revolution in 1949.

China's first national flag originated in 1872. It was yellow with a blue dragon, representing the Manchu (Qing) Dynasty, which ruled China for many years. The revolt of 1911 saw the changing of the flag to five different colored stripes. Soviet republics were established in the 1920s, each of which was represented by a red flag referring to the Soviet fatherland. The present flag dates from 1949, when the People's Republic was formed.

The large star represents communism. The red field signifies revolution and echoes the ancient Han Dynasty of 206 BC. The four stars represent the four social classes: peasants, workers, petty bourgeoisie, and patriotic capitalists.

FLAG OF HONG KONG IN 1997

FLAG OF MACAO IN 1999

North Korea

Adopted September 8, 1948 | **Ratio** 1:2 | **Usage** National and Civil

The two blue stripes stand for sovereignty, peace, and friendship

The white stripes symbolize purity

The star is a symbol of communism

Red represents the Communist revolution

The Kingdom of Korea was annexed by Japan in 1910. In 1948, the peninsula was partitioned into democratic South and Communist North Korea.

The flag was adopted in 1948, when North Korea became an independent Communist state. The traditional Korean flag was red, white, and blue. The regime retained these colors—with more prominence given to the red— and added a red star on a white disk. The disk recalls the Chinese yin-yang symbol, which is found on the flag of South Korea, and represents the opposing principles of nature. The red stripe expresses revolutionary traditions, while the red star is for communism.

The prominent theme of the Soviet-style coat of arms is industrialization, depicted with an electricity pylon and a large dam.

ARMS OF NORTH KOREA

A hydroelectric power station within a wreath of rice-ears

Industrial elements feature heavily on the arms of Korea and include a large dam and electricity pylon

The star of communism

The inscription on the scroll is the country's official name—The Democratic People's Republic of Korea

South Korea

Adopted July 12, 1948 | **Ratio** 2:3 | **Usage** National and Civil

The three unbroken bars symbolize heaven

White is the traditional color of the Korean people

This trigram represents water

This trigram represents fire

Yin-yang symbol signifies harmony and the union of opposites

The three broken bars symbolize earth

South Korea forms the southern half of the Korean Peninsula, which was partitioned close to the 38th parallel after the Second World War.

The flag used by the Kingdom of Korea before 1910 featured the traditional colors: red, white, and blue. When South Korea separated from the north in 1948, the original flag was retained, but a few alterations were made.

A NEW SOUTH KOREAN FLAG

At the flag's center is a disk containing an S-shaped line, the upper half being red, and the lower half blue. This is derived from the Eastern *yin-yang* symbol, which represents the harmony of opposites in nature, for example, good and evil; male and female. When North and South Korea separated, the shape of the *yin-yang* was stylized in the form of a

Japanese *mon*. These are simplified versions of everyday objects, shown in symmetrical and regular forms. *Yang* is represented by red, and *yin* by blue.

The other alteration to the original flag in 1948 was to the trigrams (*kwae*) surrounding the *yin-yang*, which were reduced from eight to four. They are the basic trigrams from the *I-Ching*, a divination system widespread in the East. On the South Korean flag they symbolize the four polarities: heaven (upper hoist), water (upper fly), fire (lower hoist), and earth (lower fly). The white field of the flag represents peace and the white clothing traditionally worn by the Korean people.

Japan

Adopted February 27, 1870 | **Ratio** 2:3 | **Usage** National and Civil

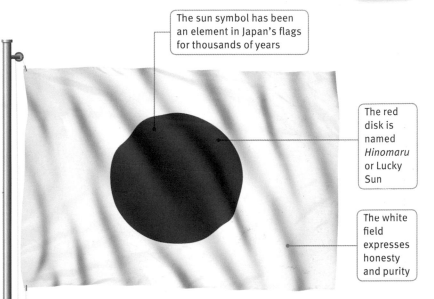

The sun symbol has been an element in Japan's flags for thousands of years

The red disk is named *Hinomaru* or Lucky Sun

The white field expresses honesty and purity

Isolated from the world for centuries, Japan began to modernize in the 19th century. After defeat in Second World War, it became a democracy.

Japan is known as "The Land of the Rising Sun." The Emperor of Japan and his predecessors descend from the House of Yamato, which united the country in AD 200, and they claim to be direct descendants of the sun goddess, Amaterasu Omikami.

The current flag was officially established as the national flag of Japan in 1870.

THE *HINOMARU*

The Lucky Sun, or *Hinomaru*, in the center of the flag, has been an imperial badge since the 14th century. The white field stands for purity and integrity, and some suggest the red disk represents brightness, sincerity, and warmth. The Japanese Maritime SDF ensign is an unusual adaptation of the national flag.

JAPANESE MARITIME SDF ENSIGN

Adopted in 1889, the naval ensign consists of the sun-disk with red rays extending to the border of the flag

Rays extend to the edge of the flag to recall the rising sun

Australasia and Oceania

Australia

Adopted September 1, 1901 | **Ratio** 1:2 | **Usage** National and Civil

The Union Jack is retained in the canton

The stars of the Southern Cross

The points of the "Commonwealth Star" represent the members of the Federation

The great southern continent of Australia was unified in 1901, as a commonwealth of six formerly separate British subject states.

The first national flag was adopted in 1901 following various design competitions, but its use was restricted. It includes a blue ensign and three motifs, celebrating key aspects of Australian statehood.

THE SOUTHERN CROSS

This constellation is visible throughout the year in southern night skies and has been used as a navigational aid for centuries. It helped guide early European ships to the continent and became a popular emblem for the new settlers. The five stars of the cross appear on the fly, with seven points for the brightest stars, and five for the lesser Epsilon Crucis.

THE UNION JACK

First flown on Australian soil by Captain Cook, it was the national flag from 1788 and remained the official citizens' land flag until 1954. It occupies the canton, denoting Australia's historical links with Great Britain.

THE "COMMONWEALTH STAR"

This large star affirms the federal nature of government in Australia. Originally there were six points for the six federal states. The seventh point was added in 1909, to represent the Northern Territory together with the six other external territories administered by the Australian Federal Government.

Australia: State flags

The state flags all use the British Blue Ensign, with the state badge in the canton. The two territories do not follow this pattern.

Australian Capital Territory

The capital territory became self-governing in 1989. The flag, adopted in 1993, depicts Canberra's city coat of arms and the Southern Cross in the city colors of blue and gold.

New South Wales

A gold star adorns each arm of the St. George's Cross, with a golden lion *passant guardant* at the center. This more distinctive badge replaced a previous design in 1876.

Northern Territory

Adopted by the territory in 1978, the flag depicts the Southern Cross and a stylized Sturt's desert rose against black and ocher, which are the territorial colors.

Queensland

The state badge depicts the Royal Crown at the center of a Maltese cross. The design of the crown was altered at the coronation of HM Queen Elizabeth II in 1953.

State flags (continued)

South Australia

The state emblem of the piping shrike (a magpie) is shown with outstretched wings on a yellow background. The piping shrike was adopted as the flag badge in 1904.

Tasmania

The Red Lion *passant* on a white background recalls historical ties with England and has remained essentially unchanged since its adoption in 1875.

Victoria

The Royal Crown was added in 1877. The present arrangement, with the crown surmounting the Southern Cross, became the state arms in 1910.

Western Australia

The Black Swan has been Western Australia's emblem since the first British colony was founded at Swan River. The flag was adopted in 1953.

Vanuatu

Adopted February 13, 1980 | **Ratio** 3:5 | **Usage** National and Civil

The boar's tusk symbolizes prosperity

Red is symbolic of blood

Green recalls the richness of the islands

The fern leaves represent peaceful intentions

The yellow Y-shape depicts the outline of the Vanuatu archipelago and the color of sunshine

Vanuatu, formerly known as the New Hebrides, was jointly administered by Britain and France from 1906. In 1980, it gained its independence.

During its time as an Anglo-French condominium, the New Hebrides flew the French *Tricolore* side by side with the Union Jack. After the anglophone Vanuaaku Party led the country to independence as Vanuatu in 1980, the colors of the party flag—red, black, green, and yellow—were adopted as the basis for the design of a new national flag. The final design was chosen a few months before independence by a parliamentary committee from designs submitted by a local artist.

THE SYMBOLISM OF THE COLORS

The yellow symbolizes sunshine; the green reflects the richness of the islands. The red is symbolic of blood, and the black is for the Melanesian people. The Prime Minister requested the inclusion of the yellow and black fimbriations to give more prominence to the color representing the people. The yellow Y-shape denotes the pattern of the islands in the Pacific Ocean.

THE BOAR'S TUSK

Between the arms of the "Y" lies the traditional emblem of a boar's tusk—the symbol of prosperity, worn as a pendant on the islands—crossed by two leaves of the local *namele* fern. The leaves are a token of peace, and their 39 fronds represent the 39 members of Vanuatu's legislative assembly.

Fiji

Adopted October 10, 1970 | **Ratio** 1:2 | **Usage** National and Civil

The Union Jack denotes the historical links with Great Britain

The design is based on the British Blue Ensign

The blue field represents the Pacific Ocean

Fiji became part of the British Empire in 1874, and an independent nation with dominion status within the Commonwealth in 1970.

The flag was adopted in 1970, when Fiji achieved independence. Its bright blue background symbolizes the Pacific Ocean, which plays an important part in the lives of the islanders, both in terms of the fishing industry, and the burgeoning tourist trade. The Union Jack reflects the country's links with Great Britain.

ARMS OF FIJI

The shield is derived from the country's official coat of arms, which was originally granted by Royal Warrant in 1908. The images depicted on the shield represent agricultural activities on the islands, and the historical associations with Great Britain.

ARMS OF FIJI

On the chief, a British lion holds a coconut between its paws

The first quarter shows sugarcane; the second, a coconut palm; the third, a dove of peace; and the fourth, a bunch of bananas

The coat of arms was granted in 1908; it is a white shield, with a red cross and a red chief (the upper third of a shield)

Papua New Guinea

Adopted July 1, 1971 | **Ratio** 3:4 | **Usage** National and Civil

The five stars represent the Southern Cross, but also refer to a local legend about five sisters

Red and black are the predominant colors in the native art of Papua New Guinea

A golden bird of paradise

Papua New Guinea gained full independence in 1975, following its status as a United Nations Trusteeship under Australian administration.

The Australian administration attempted to introduce Papua New Guinea's first official national flag in 1970. Its choice was a vertically divided flag: blue at the hoist with the stars of the Southern Cross as in the Australian flag, then white, then green with a golden bird of paradise. The proposed design was never popular with the local people.

A LOCAL DESIGN

The current flag of yellow and white symbols on black and red was designed by a 15-year-old art student, Susan Karike, and officially accepted in 1971. When Papua New Guinea became independent in 1975, it was retained as the national flag.

THE COLORS OF NATIVE ART

The colors of the field—red and black—were chosen because of their widespread use in the native art of the country. The bird of paradise has long been a local emblem, and its feathers are used for traditional dress and in festivals and ceremonies.

THE SOUTHERN CROSS

The flag is halved diagonally. The lower half features the Southern Cross constellation in white on black, as it would appear in the night sky, over Papua New Guinea. This signifies the link with Australia and also recalls a local legend about five sisters. The red upper half bears a golden bird of paradise in flight.

Solomon Islands

Adopted November 18, 1977 | **Ratio** 1:2 | **Usage** National and Civil

The five stars represent the five main groups of islands

The yellow stripe symbolizes sunshine

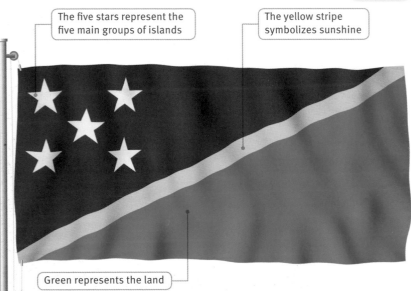

Green represents the land

The Solomon Islands were a British colony from 1883, until they became self-governing in 1976, and subsequently independent in 1978.

Before the current flag was adopted in 1977, three different coats of arms had represented the islands.

The national flag, adopted in 1977, is divided diagonally by a stripe of yellow representing the sunshine of the islands. The two triangles formed by the diagonal stripe are blue and green, signifying water and the land. The five stars were initially incorporated to represent the country's five districts. The islands were later divided into seven districts and the symbolism of the stars was modified to refer to the five main groups of islands.

The coat of arms is also in the colors of the national flag.

ARMS OF THE SOLOMON ISLANDS

The crest is a traditional canoe (in section) and a shining sun

A freshwater crocodile

The national motto— "To lead is to serve"

A shark

The shield depicts frigate birds, an eagle, two turtles, a shield and bow and arrow, all representing districts of the Solomon Islands

The compartment is a stylized frigate bird

Palau

Adopted January 1, 1981 | **Ratio** 5:8 | **Usage** National and Civil

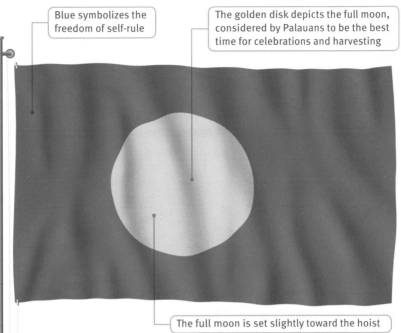

Blue symbolizes the freedom of self-rule

The golden disk depicts the full moon, considered by Palauans to be the best time for celebrations and harvesting

The full moon is set slightly toward the hoist

Under US control since 1945, Palau became a republic in 1981. In 1994, it became independent in association with the United States.

The current flag was introduced in 1981 when Palau became a republic. Previously, the flag of the Trust Territory of the Pacific Islands was flown jointly with the United Nations and United States flags.

THE SYMBOLISM OF THE FLAG
The flag's very simple design belies the depth of meaning attributed to it. The explanation for the choice of colors is rooted in the history and customs of the Palauan people. The bright blue of the field, which might be assumed to be symbolic of the Pacific Ocean, is in fact a representation of the transition from foreign domination to self-government. The golden disk, which sits slightly off center toward

the hoist, represents the full moon. The Palauans consider the full moon to be the optimum time for human activity. This time of the month when celebrations, harvesting and planting, fishing, tree-felling, and the carving of traditional canoes are carried out. The moon is a symbol of peace, love, and tranquility.

THE SEAL OF PALAU
Palau does not have a coat of arms, but has a seal, adopted in 1981, when the country became a republic. The seal is not colored. It depicts a traditional Palauan triangular hut, above the date of adoption. This is surrounded by the title of the state.

Micronesia

Adopted November 10, 1979 | **Ratio** 10:19 | **Usage** National and Civil

The light blue field recalls the Pacific Ocean

The four stars each represent an island group

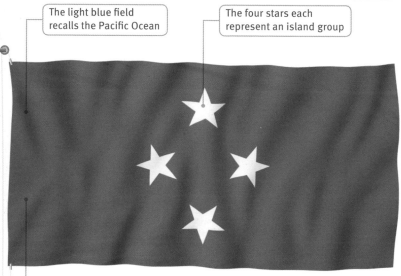

The colors are similar to those of the UN flag

Micronesia was part of the US-administered United Nations Trust Territory of the Pacific Islands, until it became independent in 1979.

The flag, adopted in 1978, is in the colors of the UN flag. The light blue also represents the Pacific Ocean.

In an echo of US practice, the stars are for the four islands, arranged like the points of the compass.

MICRONESIAN STATES

Chuuk

The white coconut palm shows that the people depend on coconut resources. The white stars represent the 38 municipal units in the territory.

Kosrae

The olive branches symbolize peace. The four stars are for the islands' four units. The *fafa* stone is traditionally used for grinding food.

Pohnpei

The 11 stars are for the district's 11 municipalities. The half coconut shell represents the *sakau* cup used in traditional ceremonies.

Yap

The outer and inner rings show a *rai*, a traditional symbol of unity. The white outrigger canoe symbolizes the desire to reach state goals.

Marshall Islands

Adopted May 1, 1979 | **Ratio** 10:19 | **Usage** National and Civil

A 24-pointed star, one for each of the districts on the islands

Blue field for the Pacific Ocean

The two stripes, orange over white, represent the two parallel chains of the Marshall Islands

The Marshall Islands were part of the US Trust Territory of the Pacific Islands from 1945–86. They became fully independent in 1990.

The Marshall Islands became a self-governing territory on May 1, 1979, and on that day a new national flag was adopted. Designed by Emlain Kabua, wife of the president of the new government, it was the winning entry in a competition that had attracted 50 designs.

A FLAG FOR A PACIFIC ISLAND

The flag's dark blue field represents the vast area of the Pacific Ocean over which the islands are scattered. The star symbolizes the geographical position of the islands, which lie a few degrees above the Equator. The star has 24 points, representing the 24 municipalities of the Marshall Islands. Four of its rays extend farther than the others and stand for the capital, Majuro, and the administrative districts of Wotji, Yaluit, and Kwajalein. They also form a cross, signifying the Christian faith of the Marshallese.

SYMBOLS OF PROSPERITY

The two parallel stripes extending across the flag symbolize the two parallel chains of the Marshall Islands: the Ratak (Sunrise) Chain is white, while the Ralik (Sunset) Chain is orange. The stripes extend and widen upward. This is said to signify the increase in growth and vitality of life on the islands. Orange also symbolizes courage and prosperity, while white represents peace.

Nauru

Adopted January 31, 1968 | **Ratio** 1:2 | **Usage** National and Civil

The blue field represents the island's blue skies and the Pacific Ocean

The gold stripe represents the Equator

The 12-pointed star recalls the 12 original tribes of Nauru

Nauru was jointly administered by Australia, the UK and New Zealand from 1947 until independence was granted in 1968.

The flag, chosen in a local design competition, was adopted on the day of independence. It depicts Nauru's geographical position, one degree below the Equator. A gold horizontal stripe representing the Equator runs across a blue field for the Pacific Ocean. Nauru itself is symbolized by a white 12-pointed star. Each point represents one of the 12 indigenous tribes on the island.

ARMS OF NAURU
This is also a local design and includes the chemical symbol for phosphorus; phosphates are Nauru's main export. Beneath it are a frigate bird and a sprig of *tomano*.

ARMS OF NAURU

The shield is surrounded by coconut leaves

The chemical symbol for phosphorus

A frigate bird

The 12-pointed star, as featured on the flag, representing the 12 tribes of Nauru

The feathers of a frigate bird

A sprig of *tomano*

Kiribati

Adopted July 12, 1979 | **Ratio** 1:2 | **Usage** National and Civil

The red shield in the coat of arms also depicts a gold flying frigate bird above a rising golden sun

The frigate bird symbolizes command of the sea

The blue and white wavy bands represent the Pacific Ocean

Once part of the British colony of the Gilbert and Ellice Islands, the Gilberts became independent in 1979 and adopted the name Kiribati.

Kiribati's flag is one of only three national flags that are armorial banners—flags having a design, which corresponds exactly to that of the shield in the coat of arms.

ARMS OF KIRIBATI

The coat of arms dates back to May 1937 when it was granted to the Gilbert and Ellice Islands, as Kiribati and Tuvalu were then known. The shield, was then incorporated into the center of the fly half of a British Blue Ensign as the state ensign of the colony.

Shortly before independence was granted in 1979, a local competition was held to choose a new national flag and a design based on the colonial coat of arms, was submitted to the College of Arms. The College of Arms decided to modify the design. Both the golden frigate bird and the sun were enlarged to occupy more of the top of the flag and the width of the blue and white wavy bands was reduced.

THE ORIGINAL DESIGN

However, the local people insisted on the original design, in which the top and bottom halves of the flag were equal, the sun and local frigate bird small, and the various design elements outlined in black.

The new flag was hoisted during the independence day celebrations in the capital, Tarawa on July 12, 1979.

Tuvalu

Adopted April 11, 1997 | **Ratio** 1:2 | **Usage** National and Civil

The Union Jack signifies continuing links with Britain

The nine stars are for the nine islands

The Ellice Islands separated from the Gilbert and Ellice Islands in 1975, and adopted the name Tuvalu. Independence was gained in 1978.

Tuvalu means "eight islands," although there are in fact nine, each of which is represented by a star on the flag. The stars' arrangement is supposed to reflect the islands' geographic distribution.

This flag was chosen because it symbolizes the continuing links with Britain and the Commonwealth.

However, anti-Commonwealth feeling rose and in 1995, the government decided on a new flag without the Union Jack. The new flag introduced later that year, retained the stars, but included the arms in a triangle at the hoist. In April 1997 the original design was readopted, following a change of government.

ARMS OF TUVALU

The coat of arms depicts a local meeting house, or *maneapa*

Eight sets of objects reflect the country's title, "Eight Together"

The border contains eight sea shells and eight banana leaves

The motto means "Tuvalu for God"

Samoa

Adopted January 1, 1962 | **Ratio** 1:2 | **Usage** National and Civil

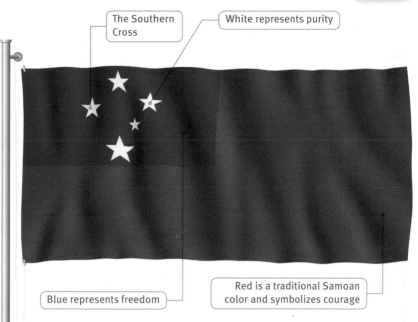

The Southern Cross

White represents purity

Blue represents freedom

Red is a traditional Samoan color and symbolizes courage

Under the administration of Germany, the US and later New Zealand, Samoa became the first independent Polynesian nation in 1962.

Prior to 1899, when Samoa was partitioned by Germany and the US, it was ruled by the rival kingdoms of Malietoa and Tamasese.

The flag of Malietoa was probably inspired by missionaries. It was a plain red field, with a white cross and a white star in the canton. The rival King of Tamasese favored the German cause and used flags with black crosses.

A UNITED FLAG

In 1948, by then a territory of New Zealand, Samoa was granted its current flag. This was created jointly by the kings of Malietoa and Tamasese. It comprised a red field taken from the former flag of Malietoa and the Southern Cross from the flag of New Zealand, on a blue field in the canton.

In 1949, the smaller fifth star was added, making the Southern Cross more like that on the Australian flag. The flag was retained when independence was granted in 1962.

ARMS OF SAMOA

The coat of arms was adopted in 1951 and contains symbols reflecting the Christian faith of the Samoan people. It depicts a shield of the Southern Cross, below a coconut palm from the previous colonial badge. Above the shield is a cross recalling the national motto—"May God be the foundation of Samoa."

Tonga

Adopted November 4, 1875 | **Ratio** 1:2 | **Usage** National and Civil

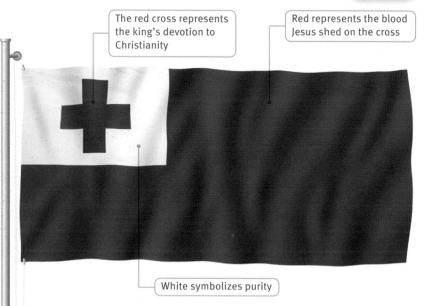

The red cross represents the king's devotion to Christianity

Red represents the blood Jesus shed on the cross

White symbolizes purity

Tonga was unified under King George Tupou I in 1820. In 1900, it became a British protectorate before regaining its independence in 1970.

The flag dates from 1862 when the king at the time, who had converted to Christianity in 1831, called for a national flag which would symbolize the Christian faith.

A NEW "CHRISTIAN" FLAG

The first design was a plain white flag with a red couped cross, but this was later found to be too similar to the International Red Cross flag, adopted in 1863, and so the white flag was placed in the canton of a red one. The cross and the red color signify the sacrifice of Christ's blood. The 1875 constitution states that the flag shall never be altered.

The naval ensign, introduced in 1985, also has a red couped cross on white in the canton.

TONGAN NAVAL ENSIGN

Red couped cross in the canton

The naval ensign, introduced in 1985, recalls the flag of Imperial Germany

A red cotised, or bordered, Scandinavian cross

New Zealand

Adopted March 24, 1902 | **Ratio** 1:2 | **Usage** National

The Union Jack in the canton recalls New Zealand's colonial ties to Britain

The stars all vary slightly in size

Four white-bordered red stars represent the Southern Cross

New Zealand was settled by the British in the 1800s and was a colony from 1841. It became a dominion in 1907 and fully independent in 1947.

New Zealand's first flag was adopted before it became a British colony. Chosen by an assembly of Maori chiefs in 1834, the flag was of a St. George's Cross with another cross in the canton, containing four stars on a blue field. After the formation of the colony in 1841, British ensigns began to be used.

A NEW NATIONAL FLAG
The current flag was designed and adopted for restricted use in 1869, and became the national flag in 1902. It is the British Blue Ensign, with a highly stylized representation of the Southern Cross constellation. It depicts only four of the five stars in the constellation.

OVERSEAS TERRITORIES

Cook Islands

The 15 stars on the fly represent the 15 main islands of the group; they are arranged in a ring to indicate that each island is of equal importance.

Niue

The link with the UK is shown by the use of the Union Jack; that with New Zealand by the four stars. The large central star represents Niue itself.

International flags and flag codes

International flags

Many international organizations have adopted flags to help raise their profile worldwide. Here is a selection of flags belonging to well-known global organizations.

United Nations (UN)

The UN is an international organization responsible for peacekeeping missions. Its flag shows olive branches which are a symbol of peace and the map represents the people of the world.

Commonwealth of Nations

The Commonwealth of Nations is an intergovernmental organization of 53 member states. The gold "C" symbol centers on a globe, emphasizing the global nature of the organization.

European Union (EU)

An economic and political union of 28 member states, the EU's flag consists of 12 gold stars on an azure field. The stars represent the European people in a circle—a symbol of unity.

African Union (AU)

The current flag of the African Union was adopted in 2010. It shows rays of light coming out of the continent, symbolizing hope; and the 53 gold stars represent the member states.

Arab League

The flag is a green field bearing the seal of the League of Arab States. The script gives the name of the organization, while the 22 links in the chain represent the original 22 members when it was formed.

Commonwealth of Independent States (CIS)

The CIS is a regional organization whose participating countries are former Soviet Republics. The poles around the sun represent the eight members who signed the treaty in 1991.

Association of Southeast Asian Nations (ASEAN)

The ASEAN is a geopolitical and economic organization made up of 10 countries in the region. The flag depicts 10 rice stalks in the middle of a red circle. The image represents prosperity.

Secretariat of the Pacific Community

An intergovernmental agency focusing on development in the Pacific region, SPC's flag bears 27 stars representing all its members. The sail and ocean recalls linkage and the sharing of ideas.

International flags (continued)

Union of South American Nations (UNASUR)

UNASUR is committed to South American integration. Its flag is navy blue and bears the organization's logo, which depicts a whirlwind symbolizing dynamism and the spirit of change.

Caribbean Community and Common Market (CARICOM)

CARICOM's main purpose is to promote economic integration among its 15 Caribbean nations. The interlocking Cs symbolize the unity of its members, and a break from its colonial past.

North Atlantic Treaty Organization (NATO)

The North Atlantic Treaty Organization's flag depicts a compass, symbolizing its endeavour to remain on a path of peace. The circle represents the unity that binds together the 14 member states.

International Maritime Organization (IMO)

The IMO's flag is based on the UN flag. It shows the world map on two crossed anchors, surrounded by laurel leaves, which symbolize the organization's knowledge of the world's oceans.

Organization of Petroleum Exporting Countries (OPEC)

The Organization of Petroleum Exporting Countries consists of 11 nations whose economy is reliant on oil revenues. The flag bears the logo, with the letters stylized to resemble oil barrels.

Red Cross, Red Crescent, Red Crystal

These are the variant flags of the global humanitarian aid organization (adopted to show religious sensitivity). The symbols serve as protective markings in armed conflicts.

Greenpeace

The largest international environmental organization in the world, Greenpeace's flag bears a rainbow over a world map, which symbolizes its determination to protect the environment by peaceful means.

International Federation of Vexillological Assoc. (FIAV)

The flag of the International Federation of Vexillological Associations depicts two halyards (ropes) forming two interlaced loops. The image symbolizes the link between all the countries of the world.

Signaling flags

Signaling at sea is one of the oldest uses of flags. Signals were sent with flaglike objects called vexilloids during the wars between the Greeks and the Persians (478–47 BCE). By the Middle Ages, the Genoese and Venetian fleets of Italy had more elaborate signals. The first specially made signal flag was the "Banner of Council" introduced for the English fleet in 1369 (used to call the captain to the admiral's ship). Signals were also sent by hoisting ordinary flags in special positions.

CODE OF SIGNALS
The first regular code of signals dates from the 17th century in England and numeral flags were invented in the 1800s. These numbers could also represent letters of the alphabet, and they were used to send messages and commands in the heat of battle. Each ship also used pennants to represent its name. In 1812, Sir Home Popham introduced special flags for letters of the alphabet, and by 1889 there was a specific flag for each letter

and numeral. The first International Code of Signals (ICS) was introduced on January 1, 1901.

INTERNATIONAL CODE OF SIGNALS (ICS) FLAGS
The purpose of this set of signals is to offer a means of communication to help mariners navigate their vessels safely. Below is a listing of the numeral or letter of the alphabet that each flag denotes.

NUMBERS

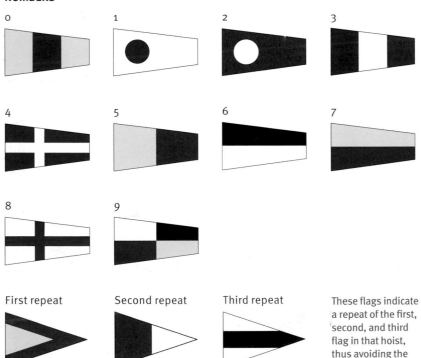

0   1   2   3

4   5   6   7

8   9

First repeat   Second repeat   Third repeat

These flags indicate a repeat of the first, second, and third flag in that hoist, thus avoiding the need for multiple sets of flags.

LETTERS

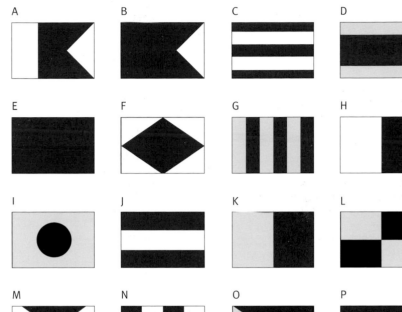

A B C D

E F G H

I J K L

M N O P

Q R S T

U V W X

Y Z

Signaling flags (continued)

SIGNAL COMBINATIONS

While each flag carries its own message —for example, hoisting flag H means "I have a pilot on board"—flags hoisted in combination convey a wide variety of different messages. These signals are internationally recognized and can be looked up in a code book held by both parties. Below is a selection of signals.

A
C

I am abandoning my vessel

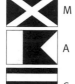

M
A
C

I request you arrange hospital admission

N
T

Distress signal

I
T

I am on fire

U
S
4

Nothing can be done until weather moderates

A
N

I need a doctor

NAVAL MANEUVRING SIGNALS

The ICS has also created a set of flags that vessels can use to indicate the maneuvers they are making and issue commands to other vessels. Some of the signs provide information of a vessel's course or an action it is about to take, while others are distress signals that prompt those nearby to keep their distance. Below are some of the most commonly used maneuvering signals.

Code/answer

Preparative

Question

Negation

Designation

Course Pennant

Turn

Smoke

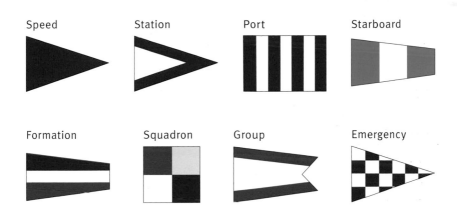

Speed | Station | Port | Starboard

Formation | Squadron | Group | Emergency

"ENGLAND EXPECTS..."

Nelson's famous signal at Trafalgar in 1805 was composed of hoists taken from Popham's *Dictionary of Signals,* except for the last word "Duty." This had to be spelled out using the numerals from an earlier official signal book. Nelson also wanted to use the word "confides," but this was also absent from the dictionary.

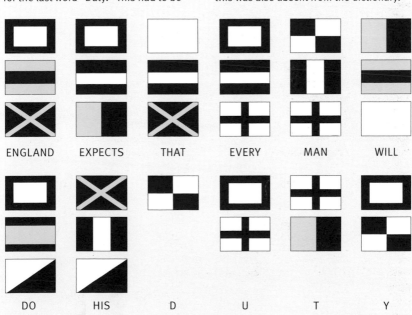

ENGLAND | EXPECTS | THAT | EVERY | MAN | WILL

DO | HIS | D | U | T | Y

Semaphore

The semaphore flag signaling system is used to convey information at a distance via visual signals with hand-held flags. It involves holding a specially designed flag in each hand and changing the positions of both arms to represent different letters and numbers. In the past semaphores were primarily used by navy vessels to communicate messages between them.

SEMAPHORES IN BATTLE

This system of signaling was routinely used during naval battles in the 19th century. Most famously, semaphores were used in the Battle of Trafalgar during the Napoleonic Wars. Nowadays, the semaphore system used at sea involves flags that are square and divided diagonally into a red and yellow color.

(The flags used on land are colored white and blue.) The skill of semaphore continues to be taught to navy signalers and they are still used occasionally, during replenishment at sea, for example. Below is a listing of the message, numeral, or character of the alphabet that each signal denotes.

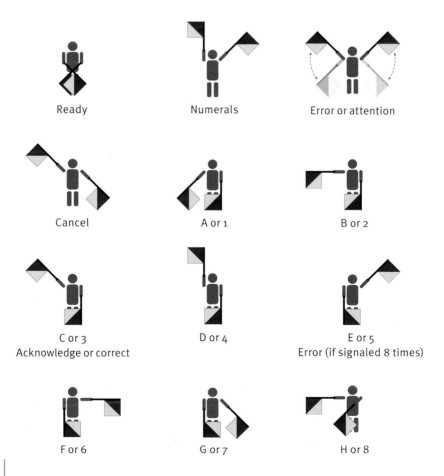

Ready

Numerals

Error or attention

Cancel

A or 1

B or 2

C or 3
Acknowledge or correct

D or 4

E or 5
Error (if signaled 8 times)

F or 6

G or 7

H or 8

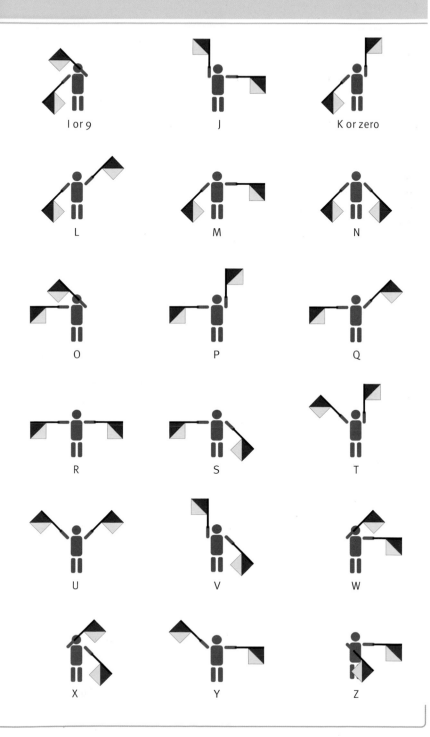

Index

Index (continued)

Acknowledgments

The publisher would like to thank the following for their kind permission to reproduce their photographs:

(Key: a-above; b-below/bottom; c-center; f-far; l-left; r-right; t-top)

1 Dreamstime.com: niroworld. **10 Dorling Kindersley:** National Maritime Museum, London (br). **12 Corbis:** Pascal Le Segretain / Sygma (b). **Dorling Kindersley:** National Maritime Museum, London (tr). **13 NASA:** Charles M. Duke Jr. / JSC (t)

All other images © Dorling Kindersley. For further information see: www.dkimages.com